LESSONS FROM THE PARTNERSHIPS FOR SOCIAL AND EMOTIONAL LEARNING INITIATIVE

VOLUME 3

D1823864

Skills for Success

Developing Social and Emotional Competencies in Out-of-School-Time Programs

JENNIFER T. LESCHITZ, SUSANNAH FAXON-MILLS,
ANDREA PRADO TUMA, KATIE TOSH,
CATHERINE H. AUGUSTINE, HEATHER L. SCHWARTZ

Commissioned by

For more information on this publication, visit **www.rand.org/t/RRA379-11**.

About RAND

The RAND Corporation is a research organization that develops solutions to public policy challenges to help make communities throughout the world safer and more secure, healthier and more prosperous. RAND is nonprofit, nonpartisan, and committed to the public interest. To learn more about RAND, visit www.rand.org.

Research Integrity

Our mission to help improve policy and decisionmaking through research and analysis is enabled through our core values of quality and objectivity and our unwavering commitment to the highest level of integrity and ethical behavior. To help ensure our research and analysis are rigorous, objective, and nonpartisan, we subject our research publications to a robust and exacting quality-assurance process; avoid both the appearance and reality of financial and other conflicts of interest through staff training, project screening, and a policy of mandatory disclosure; and pursue transparency in our research engagements through our commitment to the open publication of our research findings and recommendations, disclosure of the source of funding of published research, and policies to ensure intellectual independence. For more information, visit www.rand.org/about/research-integrity.

RAND's publications do not necessarily reflect the opinions of its research clients and sponsors.

ABOUT THIS REPORT

This report offers practical guidance for out-of-school-time (OST) programs and out-of-school-time intermediaries that wish to incorporate social and emotional learning (SEL) activities into their programming for youth. The lessons are derived from RAND's study over four years of more than 100 afterschool programs across six communities participating in The Wallace Foundation's Partnerships for Social and Emotional Learning Initiative (PSELI).

The Wallace Foundation designed PSELI to explore whether and how children benefit when schools and OST programs partner to improve and coordinate SEL programming, as well as what it takes to do this work. The six communities involved in PSELI are Boston, Massachusetts; Dallas, Texas; Denver, Colorado; Palm Beach County, Florida; Tacoma, Washington; and Tulsa, Oklahoma.

RAND Education and Labor

This study was undertaken by RAND Education and Labor, a division of the RAND Corporation that conducts research on early childhood through postsecondary education programs, workforce development, and programs and policies affecting workers, entrepreneurship, and financial literacy and decisionmaking.

This study was sponsored by The Wallace Foundation, which seeks to foster equity and improvements in learning and enrichment for young people and in the arts for everyone. For more information and research on these and other related topics, please visit its Knowledge Center at www.wallacefoundation.org.

More information about RAND can be found at www.rand.org. Questions about this report should be directed to Jennifer T. Leschitz at jtamargo@rand.org, and questions about RAND Education and Labor should be directed to educationandlabor@ rand.org.

Acknowledgments

We thank the out-of-school-time and out-of-school-time intermediary program staff who spent their time providing us information about their work. They were generous with their time. We also thank The Wallace Foundation staff, as well as partners from the Collaborative for Academic, Social, and Emotional Learning and the Forum for Youth Investment's Weikart Center for Youth Program Quality, for carefully reviewing drafts of this report and helping improve it. We are especially grateful to Ann Stone at The Wallace Foundation for her support and guidance throughout this project. Michelle Bongard, Brittany Joseph, Rebecca Lawrence, and Sarah Weilant all contributed to the report through coding of interviews or data analysis. This report benefited substantively from feedback from our quality assurance manager, Katie Carman, and from our reviewers, Becki Herman and Richard Fournier. We are grateful for their careful reviews and constructive feedback. Finally, we appreciate the expert editing and publications team at RAND, including Nora Spiering, Katherine Wu, and Monette Velasco. Any flaws that remain are solely the authors' responsibility.

SUMMARY

Strengthening children's social and emotional skills can lead to better learning, health, and well-being. Out-of-school-time (OST) programs have long focused on children's social and emotional development and engage in social and emotional learning (SEL) work as part of their mission of building a culture of connectedness and positive relationships between youth and adults. Research demonstrates that high-quality, evidence-based SEL programs are associated with positive outcomes, including improved behavior, attitudes, and academic performance.

This report provides tips and recommendations for incorporating high-quality SEL instruction and practices into OST programming for children and youth. To develop these tips and recommendations, we drew on an extensive set of data, including surveys, interviews, observations, and document reviews from more than 100 OST programs (primarily afterschool programs) across six communities—Boston, Dallas, Denver, Palm Beach County, Tacoma, and Tulsa—participating in The Wallace Foundation's Partnerships for Social and Emotional Learning Initiative.

We aim for this report to be particularly useful for OST practitioners and out-of-school-time intermediaries (OSTIs), which are organizations that provide support and services (e.g., professional development, data analysis) to individual OST programs in a given community. The report summarizes a variety of approaches and actions that OST programs developed over four years to support children's social-emotional development, including adding SEL content and practices into their programming, training staff in SEL, engaging families, and adopting continuous improvement systems to monitor and refine these efforts.

Although the programs that we profile tackled challenges that OST programs across the United States commonly face, such as frequent staff turnover, these programs were also distinct because they participated in a philanthropically funded initiative that explores how schools and OST programs can partner to develop and implement intensive mutually reinforcing SEL activities to improve climate (e.g., program space, values, practices) and support children's SEL. Each OST program that we profile received grant funds, training, and organizational resources from an OSTI that was participating in the initiative. Therefore, we also summarize the many ways in which OSTIs or similar organizations can support OST programs in their SEL programming for children and youth.

In addition to the tips for success featured throughout the report, we offer the following recommendations for OST program and OSTI leaders:

- **Phase in SEL instruction over time.** Start with a few easy-to-enact SEL rituals, then add in moments of SEL instruction into regular program activities, and finally graduate to stand-alone SEL lessons derived from a curriculum. Rather than launching everything at once, it helps for OST programs to start with small goals and allow OST instructors to accrue experience teaching SEL to youth over time.

- **Deliver multiple SEL professional development opportunities spread throughout the year.** Start with a longer kick-off training and follow up with short sessions, all of which include opportunities for development of adult SEL skills, modeling, and practice. Written onboarding materials about SEL, easily accessible and repeatable SEL trainings at multiple timepoints, differentiated professional development, and payment to attend professional development can each help address the ongoing challenge of training a workforce that has high rates of turnover.

- **Engage with families about SEL using multiple forms of outreach.** OST programs were more successful when they used multiple outreach methods to share information about SEL with families and guardians such as program calendars, websites, email, bulletin boards, and in-person contact. Some OST programs also had success including families in SEL-themed activities at family nights and providing SEL activities for families to try at home.

- **Track SEL implementation as part of a continuous quality improvement cycle.** Start by collecting a narrow set of data and reviewing it in a recurring cycle that leads to steps for program improvement. Clearly defined SEL goals can help programs and OSTIs to identify areas of focus and guide data collection efforts. In addition, scheduling data use cycles, developing action plans, and holding regular meetings to review data can help create accountability and support program improvement.

- **OSTIs—or other similar organizations, such as mayor's offices, district afterschool offices, or youth-based networks—can work with OST programs that need support in order to offer SEL activities.** OSTIs and the like can help fill gaps in OST program capacity—for example, by developing SEL lessons for OST instructors, leading a continuous quality improvement process, or creating a SEL professional development sequence.

Contents

CHAPTER ONE

Background

Strengthening children's social and emotional skills can lead to better learning, health, and well-being.[1] These positive benefits appear to be durable. Research documents benefits in education, employment, criminal activity, substance use, and mental health domains years after social and emotional development in early childhood.[2] Such competencies as empathy, self-awareness, and responsible decisionmaking can also advance equity (e.g., by helping children and adults self-reflect on their personal biases and engage in efforts to improve community well-being).[3]

Out-of-school-time (OST) programs have long focused on children's social and emotional development. Although OST programs might not use the term, many are, in fact, engaged in social and emotional learning (SEL) work as part of their mission of building a culture of connectedness and positive relationships between youth and adults.[4] Many OST program activities offer opportunities for youth to foster relationships with adults and with peers that can support the development of SEL skills.[5] When participating in sports, drama, and the arts, for example, youth in OST programs often need to actively collaborate with each other and develop such skills as teamwork and expressing one's emotions productively. Many parents and guardians also look to OST programs to build their children's SEL skills; in a nationally representative

What Are OST Programs and OSTIs?

Out-of-school-time (OST) programs include before-school, afterschool, and summer programs. They can focus on a theme, such as science or art, or they can offer a variety of activities, including supervised time for homework or free play.

A wide variety of providers run OST programs, including nonprofit and for-profit organizations and some school districts. They range in size from small, community-based organizations to large national organizations like the Boys & Girls Clubs of America. They are funded primarily by parent fees, but some also receive public funding, such as 21st Century Community Learning Center grants, or philanthropic investments from such organizations as the United Way.

Out-of-school-time intermediaries (OSTIs) serve networking and coordinating functions, linking local OST programs across a community. OSTIs most commonly provide such services as professional learning opportunities and access to data management systems, though some directly fund and oversee OST programs. Not every community has an OSTI. However, many different types of organizations, such as nonprofit community-based organizations and city and county agencies, can offer supports that are similar to those offered by OSTIs.

2021 survey, parents and guardians said that they expected their children to develop social skills, such as teamwork, confidence, leadership, and perseverance, in OST programs.[6]

Although there is no consensus definition of SEL, the OST programs that we studied for this report adopted the Collaborative for Academic, Social, and Emotional Learning's (CASEL's) definition. CASEL defines SEL as a "process through which young people and adults acquire and apply the knowledge, skills, and attitudes to develop healthy identities, manage emotions and achieve personal and collective goals, feel and show empathy for others, establish and maintain supportive relationships, and make responsible and caring decisions."[7]

We use the term *SEL* throughout this report because it is the term used by the programs we studied. However, we note for the reader that OST programs and schools often use different terms for SEL or SEL-adjacent instruction. These different terms include *life skills*, *noncognitive skills*, *character education*, *soft skills*, and *21st-century skills*. Although they are not all the same, most focus on an overlapping set of youth skills, such as goal-setting, expressing and controlling emotions, exerting leadership, responsible decisionmaking, and empathizing with others.[8]

The quality of SEL implementation matters. By *implementation*, we mean OST programs' use of SEL rituals with youth, their delivery of stand-alone SEL lessons, and the integration of SEL instruction or instructional strategies into regular OST programming. Research demonstrates that high-quality, evidence-based SEL implementation is associated with positive outcomes, including improved behavior, attitudes, and academic performance.[9] We also know from the literature that there are several important ingredients of quality implementation: dedicating sufficient time to SEL; having opportunities for youth to practice SEL skills; staff training, buy-in, and ownership; and using data to inform decisionmaking.[10]

Focus of This Report

This report is intended for OST and out-of-school-time intermediaries (OSTI) practitioners, as well as the organizations that support them. We provide tips and recommendations for high-quality SEL implementation in OST programs. This report is one of several RAND Corporation reports about the Partnerships for Social and Emotional Learning Initiative (PSELI). We focus in this report exclusively on how OST programs implemented SEL programming and practices over the four years of PSELI (the four school years from 2017–2018 to 2020–2021). In other reports, we examine school-OST partnerships, feature case studies of individual school–OST program partnerships, and focus on school-day implementation of SEL.

To develop our recommendations, we drew on an extensive set of OST program staff surveys, observations of OST activities (e.g., arts, sports, homework, snack), interviews with OST program staff and OSTI leaders and coaches, and document reviews of programming from more than 100 OST programs across the six communities during the 2017–2018 to 2020–2021 school years. For a more detailed description of our methods and the data we collected, please see the technical appendix to our 2020 report, *Early Lessons from Schools and Out-of-School Time Programs Implementing Social and Emotional Learning* (www.rand.org/t/RRA379-1).[11] Although we drew on a wealth of data for the recommendations provided in this report, we have not yet conducted analyses to examine the relationship between SEL implementation and changes in children's SEL skills and academic achievement. These topics are the focus of a forthcoming 2024 report.

Overview of OST Programs and OSTIs in PSELI

In this section, we describe how OST programs in six communities across the United States—Boston, Massachusetts; Dallas, Texas; Denver, Colorado; Palm Beach County, Florida; Tacoma, Washington; and Tulsa, Oklahoma—pioneered SEL implementation at a time when there were no SEL curricula specifically designed for OST programs. Their SEL work most commonly consisted of helping children recognize and manage their emotions, as well as understand and empathize with others. Such skills are critical to building relationships with peers and adults.[12]

Although the programs that we profile tackled challenges common to many OST programs, such as frequent staff turnover, they were also distinct in that they participated in a philanthropically funded initiative through which they partnered with elementary schools to offer mutually reinforcing SEL programming to youth during school hours and in afterschool programming. In each of the six communities in PSELI, an OSTI disbursed grant funding over four years to the participating OST programs and provided programs with other types of supports, such as professional development (PD), access to resources, and processes for improvement. The OSTIs were Boston After School & Beyond, Big Thought (Dallas), the Denver Afterschool Alliance, Prime Time Palm Beach County, the Greater Tacoma Community Foundation, and The Opportunity Project (Tulsa).

The more than 100 OST programs that we examined in this report largely served grade K–5 youth after school. The types of programs included school district-run programs, local community-based programs that were only available within a given community (e.g., Boston Scores, Tacoma Arts Live, Dallas Park and Recreation), and national programs available nationwide (like the YMCA; see Table 1.1). Programs typically enrolled 5 to 20 percent of their school partner's enrollees, and programming typically occurred on a school campus, with hours ranging from one lunch period per week to several afterschool hours each weekday. Program activity offerings differed, but the most common combination was arts, homework help, crafts, and sports.

The structure and context of each OSTI also varied widely. For example, Boston After School & Beyond, Big Thought in Dallas, and Prime Time in Palm Beach County were all well-established, independent nonprofits that brought SEL into the fold of the supports that they had already been providing to OST programs for years. The Opportunity Project in Tulsa, on the other hand, started in the 2017–2018 school year for the initial purpose of advancing SEL through PSELI. Tacoma also did not have an established OSTI at the outset of the 2017–2018 school year, and the Greater Tacoma Community Foundation temporarily took on the role and functions of an OSTI for all four years of implementation (for the sake of brevity, we refer to it as one of the OSTIs). Denver's OSTI (the Denver Afterschool Alliance) resides within the city government rather than operating as a stand-alone organization.

Outline of This Report

In the rest of the report, we describe OST programs' approaches to infusing SEL into their programming, how they trained staff to do so, and how they enacted continuous quality improvements to their work. We also discuss how the OST programs that we studied engaged families in their SEL efforts and the ways that OSTIs

TABLE 1.1
PSELI OST Programs and OSTI Partnerships

	Boston	Dallas	Denver	Palm Beach County	Tacoma	Tulsa
Number of OST programs participating in PSELI[a]	11–26	7	6	7	21–71	5–6
OST program types[b]	District-run, community-based, national	District-run, community-based	District-run, community-based, national	District-run, community-based	District-run, community-based, national	District-run, community-based, national
OSTI	Boston After School & Beyond	Big Thought	Denver Afterschool Alliance	Prime Time Palm Beach County	Greater Tacoma Community Foundation[c]	The Opportunity Project
Year the OSTI was founded	2005	1987	2012	2000	--	2017
OSTI directly operates one or more OST programs	No	Yes	No	No	--	No

NOTE: Data shown are from spring 2018 through spring 2020 prior to coronavirus disease 2019 (COVID-19) pandemic closures.

[a] The number of participating OST programs fluctuated from year to year in Boston, Tacoma, and Tulsa.
[b] *Community-based* refers to programs only available within the community, such as Boston Scores, Tacoma Arts Live, and Youth At Heart Tulsa (among others), as opposed to national programs that are available nationwide, such as the YMCA, Playworks, Girls on the Run, and Boys & Girls Clubs of America.
[c] During the period we studied, the Greater Tacoma Community Foundation coordinated the OST programs in lieu of an OSTI.

in the six PSELI communities supported their participating OST programs in carrying out their SEL work.

To provide actionable information for readers, we have included tips for success throughout the report based on our analysis of OST programs' work, and we conclude with a series of recommendations for both OST and OSTI leaders. In the future, we will also publish a how-to guide for schools and OST programs, districts, and OSTIs that will include examples and resources for programs.

Throughout this report, unless otherwise noted, we will use *OST instructor* to refer to those program staff members who work

directly with youth, *OST program manager* to refer to those who lead or coordinate OST activities at the site or campus level, and *OST program director* for those who lead or coordinate OST program activities at the system level (e.g., across multiple sites or via an OSTI). We use the term *OST program staff* when referring to multiple roles at once.

We note that this study included only OST programs that partnered with elementary schools in urban districts and that primarily offered afterschool programming (and not summer programming or before-school programming) to youth in grades K–5. Although we studied a large number of OST programs (more than 100) that varied considerably in size and programmatic focus, it is still possible that the lessons we learned might not hold for OST programs that are different in important ways, such as serving rural areas, working independently of school partners, or being focused primarily on summer. As noted above, the OST programs that we studied also had support from a local OSTI that focused on SEL implementation; therefore, we caution that some of the tips and recommendations may need to be pared down to fit the capacity of OST programs with more-limited resources.

CHAPTER TWO

Infusing SEL Practices into OST Programming for Youth

When the OST programs and OSTIs joined PSELI, there were no off-the-shelf SEL curricula expressly designed for OST programs to embed in their own programs. As a result, most of these OST programs and OSTIs developed their own SEL content or did so in collaboration with their school partners.

The OST programs that we studied undertook SEL activities that fell along a spectrum, ranging from short SEL rituals to short, unscripted moments of SEL instruction integrated into regular OST activities to full scripted lessons as long as 30 minutes. We categorized the types of SEL activities that we observed into three types: short SEL rituals, SEL integration, and stand-alone SEL lessons (defined in the "Key SEL Terms" box).

None of the OST programs we studied enacted all three types of SEL activities immediately. Instead, they gradually added activities, as we

Key SEL Terms

Short SEL rituals: Brief activities implemented routinely during OST programming that help build a positive climate in which youth feel welcomed and valued and/or target the development of SEL skills. Examples include warmly greeting youth by name or asking them how they are feeling as they enter the OST space.

SEL integration: Either (1) embedding instruction about SEL-related topics within regular OST activities, such as an instructor pausing a basketball lesson to teach strategies about how to persist through frustration, or (2) enacting instructional strategies during regular OST activities that explicitly support SEL skill development, such as talking to children about how to work productively with one another in a group assignment.

Stand-alone SEL lessons: Dedicated time in an OST schedule when OST staff deliver a formal lesson that explicitly targets SEL topics, such as relationship skills or identifying one's emotions. These lessons can include the use of SEL lesson plans and pacing guides.

SEL lesson plans: Formal, written lessons to guide explicit SEL instruction of a group of youth.

SEL pacing guide: A document intended to support consistency in SEL instruction by outlining the sequence of SEL topics, typically by unit and weekly focus.

will describe in this section. We also provide examples of what each of these SEL activities looked like in practice and how OST programs allotted time for their SEL-focused activities.

Although additional research is needed to determine what combination of these three types of SEL activities is needed most to improve children's SEL skills or other youth outcomes, prior research from other settings points to the benefits of each activity type, as we detail in this section. Next, we describe why OST programs that are new to SEL might want to use short SEL rituals as a first step, why OST programs are well suited for SEL integration, and why it might be important to delay implementation of stand-alone SEL lessons until OST instructors are adequately trained. Of course, OST program context should inform which SEL practices to adopt. For example, including brain breaks is more relevant during homework sessions than during sports practice. And delivering stand-alone SEL lessons may not be feasible in programs that have short operating hours.

Short SEL Rituals Were Easy to Implement and Widely Used

OST programs used short SEL rituals to build a positive climate in which youth feel welcomed and valued and to target the development of SEL skills. All the OST programs across the six communities that we studied used short SEL rituals regularly, according to our interviews. In five communities, the OST programs adopted CASEL's three signature practices as their SEL rituals:

1. **warm welcomes**, such as greeting each child by name and asking them how they are feeling that day or holding morning meetings

2. **engaging practices**, such as taking a brief brain break to stand and stretch, providing clear guidance to help youth shift between activities or tasks (e.g., calming transitions), or asking youth to share their answers to a question with a partner or the larger group (e.g., sharing circles)

3. **optimistic closures**, such as using a reflective prompt to ask youth to identify what they learned that day.[13]

In the sixth community, Tacoma, OST programs adopted their own three SEL rituals: warm welcomes, emotion check-ins (in which youth talk about how they are feeling at the beginning or end of an activity), and community circles (in which youth and the instructor sit in a circle and talk about a prompt that the instructor provides that is usually related to building community, such as sharing about specific experiences, feelings, or reflections).

Several benefits are associated with these rituals. Practices like greeting all youth as they enter the space or discussing personal challenges in a community circle can help build relationships and relationship skills.[14] Short SEL rituals are also easy to implement because they can occur at any time in the program day, can be used by any OST program staff member, and take only a short amount of time.[15] The regular use of SEL rituals is associated with creating a sense of security for youth by helping them know what to expect, as well as fostering a sense of connectedness to a particular place (such as an OST program).[16] As one OST program instructor explained:

> I definitely feel like [the warm welcomes and other SEL rituals] are relationship-builders, not only with the students but with the families. It makes [students and families] feel like this is a safe environment and that I have the best intention for their child.

The OST staff members that we observed used these rituals across a wide array of activities, such as homework help sessions, drama classes, and sports activities. In 2019–2020, the most recent year in which we directly observed OST programming, we observed 197 OST program activity sessions across the six communities and noted whether OST staff used one or more of five types of SEL rituals. We observed the use of at least one SEL ritual in 56 percent of the sessions. In the hundreds of OST activity sessions that we observed over several years, OST instructors used the following rituals, ordered from most to least common.

Most common: **Calming transitions** are intended to help youth build self-regulation and emotion management skills as they shift between activities or tasks, such as transitioning from an independent learning task to group work or from recess to a new activity. By helping youth transition from one activity to the next, calming transitions can also reduce time off task, which increased time on task and engaged learning.[17] We observed OST instructors providing a countdown of minutes left to finish a particular activity or task, often while pointing to the plan for the day on a white board to give youth advance notice that they would be soon switching to a new activity. Other examples of calming transitions involve simply letting youth know that they have a certain number of minutes left to finish a task or before the end of an activity and asking youth to engage in particular behaviors to signal their readiness for a new activity, such as raising their hand or moving from sitting at their desks to sitting in a circle on the floor.

Warm welcomes are intended to create predictability for youth at the start of an activity, make youth feel that they belong and are connected to peers and staff, and encourage participation from all youth.[18] They also give instructors a way to check in and know which youth are struggling that day and should be followed up with later. We observed staff greeting youth at arrival, either just by name or with individualized actions, such as a specific handshake. We also observed group activities like a welcome song and dance, such as "Hello neighbor, what d'ya say, it's gonna be a wonderful day. So, clap your hands and boogie on down, give a little jump and turn around."

Optimistic closures can help reinforce learning for youth and provide opportunities for reflection on the day's activities.[19] The optimistic closures that we observed most often involved staff asking youth to reflect on a specific activity (e.g., how they felt during or after that activity) or lessons learned that day. A less common optimistic closure activity sometimes involved recognizing what youth had done well by, for example, doing shout-outs to highlight achievements.

Sharing circles are intended to build a sense of belonging, trusting relationships, and communication skills and create an inclusive space for youth voices.[20] Most of the sharing circles that we observed involved asking youth to sit in a circle and take turns answering a particular question posed by the instructor, such as "What are you looking forward to this week?" or "What does respectful behavior look like?" In about a third of the sharing circles that we observed, youth answered questions about their emotions, such as "What made you feel happy and sad today?" or "When do you feel confident?"

Least common: **Brain breaks** provide opportunities for youth to regain focus, usually via physical movement, such as a moment to stand up and jump around or a calming activity like deep breaths. These short breaks are supposed to help participants feel refreshed and open to learning.[21] One type of brain break consisted of games that involved some type of physical activity, such as Simon

Says, Hokey Pokey, or "getting the wiggles out." The second type involved mindfulness and breathing exercises, such as asking youth to close their eyes and feel their belly rising and falling as they breathe in and out.

TIPS FOR SUCCESS

Short SEL Rituals

Include all types of OST program staff in training on short SEL rituals—not just instructors. Short SEL rituals can be implemented throughout the program and during all OST activities so that all staff can benefit from receiving training and guidance on how to use them. For example, OST managers, instructors, and volunteers can learn to use warm welcomes when starting a new activity or when welcoming youth to the program.

Provide a brief training on short SEL rituals. A brief training on short SEL rituals can be sufficient if it provides examples, models use of the rituals, allows trainees to practice them, and provides explicit examples of how to adapt them to children of different backgrounds or levels (such as children of different ages) and situations (e.g., during snack time, during homework help). In addition, offering training on a recurring basis helps to ensure that new staff who join midyear get trained. It can also be helpful to use SEL rituals during staff meetings to model this practice for staff and encourage adult practice.

Provide OST instructors with a range of prompts and questions to guide SEL rituals that are adapted for older and younger ages so that instructors do not have to think of their own. Although OST instructors generally reported that short SEL routines were easy to implement, they also mentioned that it was hard to come up with different questions and prompts for sharing circles or warm welcomes for each day that were engaging for youth in different age groups.

Carefully consider the timing of optimistic closures. Because children often leave before closing time, adapt the timing of optimistic closures. For example, OST instructors could use optimistic closures at the end of particular activities rather than at the end of the program day. They can also use closing rituals multiple times during programming, such as at the end of each activity.

OST Staff Frequently Integrated SEL by Using Instructional Strategies to Develop SEL Skills and Making Connections to SEL Topics

We define *SEL integration* as either of two types of activities: (1) using instructional strategies to explicitly develop SEL skills, such as teaching children how to work well with one another before taking on a group task, and (2) making explicit connections to SEL topics during regular OST activities like an arts class. As with SEL rituals, integration of SEL can work well across highly varied activities, such as sports, theater, science, English language arts, and math.[22] Across all six communities that we studied, we observed that SEL integration into OST activities most commonly happened during visual or performing arts, physical education or sports, and other activities, such as cooking or computer class. It was less common in homework help and science.

The two types of SEL integration (using SEL-promoting instructional strategies and making connections to SEL topics) are not mutually exclusive; OST activities can include elements of both. For example, after an instructor sets children up for a group activity by talking through rules of productive teamwork (SEL instructional strategy), children could discuss how a character in a story felt and why (SEL topic). Although these two types of SEL integration can occur simultaneously, in the following paragraphs, we describe each of them separately in more detail.

Research suggests that there are several SEL-promoting instructional strategies, including creating opportunities for youth to take on specific responsibilities and make choices about their learning (e.g., by allowing youth to choose between different activities), collaborate with their peers to work toward a shared goal, or participate in group discussion and shared reflection.[23] Using SEL-promoting instructional strategies was not new to OST program staff; many reported using them before launching their SEL efforts. We often[a] saw youth choosing activities in which they wanted to participate, which is one instructional strategy that can develop youth leadership skills and motivation by encouraging ownership over their learning.[24] We provide examples of how programs applied these SEL-promoting instructional strategies in Table 2.1.

---

[a] In the 2019–2020 school year, we saw OST instructors creating opportunities for youth to engage in active collaboration or providing youth choice in 46 percent of the OST program activity sessions that we observed.

TABLE 2.1

SEL Integration in Action: Using SEL-Promoting Instructional Strategies

Provide opportunities for active collaboration		Youth play games or sports that require active collaboration between team members, such as soccer or collaborative board games.
		Instructors assign youth to complete a team task, such as building a structure together or creating a group art project, and discuss how to work as a team.
		Youth participate in performing arts activities that require collaboration, such as practicing and performing group songs, dance routines, and plays or videos.
Include youth voices in decisionmaking		Instructors ask youth what activities they want to participate in, such as whether to attend a cooking class or play soccer.

Making explicit connections to SEL topics during regular OST activities is the second approach to integrating SEL that we observed. For example, discussing perseverance while youth complete a task can help them persist despite experiencing frustration.[25] One OST manager explained how they incorporated reflection on SEL competencies, such as communication skills, during their sports practice:

> We incorporated recognition pins [during all our sports practice], and students are able to earn those pins throughout the season, and then, when that happens, the coach has a small team ceremony, presents the pin to the student, and [they reflect on the] explicit reasons why that person has earned the pin. . . . Are they showing positive communication skills? Are students being supportive of their teammates? Are they leading activities? Are they the first ones to raise their hands to volunteer?

We observed instructors making connections to SEL topics, as described in Table 2.2. Of the 12 SEL topics we looked for,[b] OST instructors most often made connections to the following six (in

---

[b] The 12 topics that we looked for were collaboration, growth mindset, naming emotions, naming one's own emotions, emotion regulation, cognitive regulation, empathy, diversity appreciation, conflict resolution, relationship skills, consequences, and ethical decisionmaking.

TABLE 2.2

SEL Integration in Action: Making Connections to SEL Topics

SEL Topic	Examples
Emotions	• Staff ask youth how a fictional character in a story might feel or ask them to show different emotions through movement or pictures.
	• Staff ask youth to imagine how someone might feel if they were not invited by their classmates to participate in a game.
One's own emotions	• Staff lead an emotion check-in in which youth label their emotions and describe why or how they are feeling that way.
	• Staff ask youth to describe when they felt a particular emotion.
Emotion regulation	• Staff lead youth through relaxation techniques and activities, such as deep breathing or yoga.
	• Staff lead a discussion with youth about how one can respond or react when dealing with a strong emotion, such as frustration or disappointment.
Relationship skills	• Staff ask youth to discuss why turn-taking is important when playing a board game.
	• Staff ask youth to reflect on what contributes to a successful class or activity, such as respect and listening skills.
Collaboration	• Staff explain or ask youth to reflect on instructions or rules related to teamwork and collaboration.
	• Staff explain or ask youth to reflect on what makes for good teamwork in a group activity.
Cognitive regulation	• Youth play a game to help them with impulse control and paying attention, such as Red Light/Green Light or Simon Says.
	• Youth complete an activity that requires setting goals and step-by-step planning, and then the instructor facilitates reflection on the process.
	• Staff describe class rules related to self-control, such as raising hands when youth want to talk or listening when someone else is talking.

descending order): recognizing emotions, recognizing one's own emotions, regulating emotions, developing relationship skills, building collaboration, and regulating cognition (an individual's ability to exert control over their attention, thoughts, and behaviors to achieve a goal).

We noted in our observations that OST instructors in Boston, Palm Beach County, Tacoma, and Tulsa (four of the six PSELI communities) made connections to SEL topics during OST program activity sessions more frequently over time—for example, by asking youth to make a responsible decision to share materials with other youth or asking youth to reflect on their emotions during activities. Specifically, by 2019–2020, we observed OST instructors in these four communities making connections to SEL topics in 28 percent of observed OST program activity sessions, compared with 17 percent of sessions in spring 2019. In Dallas and Denver, we saw less frequent connections to SEL topics in the 2019–2020 school year than we did in spring 2019, but this decrease could be due to an emphasis in these two communities on providing explicit SEL instruction during stand-alone SEL lessons (which we describe in the next section).

TIPS FOR SUCCESS

SEL Integration

Provide training that includes concrete examples and opportunities to model and practice SEL integration. As with training on short SEL rituals, ensure that training includes modeling of SEL integration and repeated opportunities for practice. This can help address inconsistent understanding across staff about how to incorporate SEL into their existing activities. In several communities, new staff often had a hard time learning how to integrate SEL without first receiving this type of training.

Provide OST staff with explicit documentation about how they can integrate SEL. For example, the Dallas OSTI developed guidance for integrating SEL into activities by creating connecting questions that OST instructors could use to link OST activities with an SEL theme of the week. For example, if one week's SEL theme is resilience, a connecting question that an instructor could use when youth finish working on a challenging project is "How did you show resilience?"

Ask OST instructors to explicitly discuss or write down how they will integrate SEL into activities. Although OST instructors reported that SEL integration was easy to implement during a variety of different activities, several also indicated that they forgot to do so. By creating routines for instructors, such as discussing during planning meetings how the week's activities will integrate SEL, OST managers can help ensure that SEL integration happens consistently. For example, one program required all OST instructors to identify an SEL focus in their written OST activity plans each week.

OST Instructors Least Frequently Delivered Formal Stand-Alone SEL Lessons, Which Often Included the Use of SEL Lesson Plans and Pacing Guides

Partly due to a lack of commercial SEL instructional materials designed for OST programs,[c] delivery of stand-alone SEL lessons was the least frequent of the three types of SEL activities that we observed. It did, however, become more common over time in Dallas, Denver, and Palm Beach County.

Often with help from their OSTI, the OST programs that we studied typically developed their own lessons, used pilot versions of the OST SEL programs that The Wallace Foundation sponsored, or adapted lesson plans from SEL materials designed for schools. Programs typically scheduled these stand-alone lessons during newly created "afternoon meetings" or "SEL blocks" scheduled to occur once or multiple times a week. Stand-alone SEL lessons most often focused on the same six SEL topics frequently covered during instances of SEL integration (in descending order of frequency): recognizing emotions, recognizing one's own emotions, regulating emotions, collaborating, developing relationship skills, and regulating cognition (e.g., controlling impulses, setting goals).

Stand-alone SEL lessons often involved the use of a written curriculum that had a lesson plan for the SEL activity and a pacing guide for the frequency and sequencing of the activities. An important benefit of using a curriculum is its inclusion of explicit learning goals that target specific skills, sequenced activities that provide step-by-step instruction, and suggestions for time allocations to help an OST instructor pace the lesson.[26] One OST program manager explained the benefits that they saw in using SEL curriculum:

> We really appreciate how the [curriculum] is structured, the objectives are listed out, [it includes] games. Sometimes they list options so it gives us more of a foundation to start. Our staff run typically on the younger side, some in high school, some just getting into college, universities. So the whole idea of planning a curriculum [from scratch] is a big ask for them. So having the curriculum [is helpful; it provides step-by-step guidance for our staff].

---

[c] The Wallace Foundation aimed to address the lack of SEL curricula and programs expressly for OST settings by sponsoring development of curricula and programs by the Yale Center for Emotional Intelligence, which created the RULER (Recognizing, Understanding, Labeling, Expressing, and Regulating) approach to SEL, and Committee for Children, which created the Second Step family of SEL programs.

Dallas OSTI's SEL Pacing Guide

The Dallas OSTI's SEL pacing guide followed a weekly theme (e.g., "empathy"), and each week's lessons consisted of four parts:

1. one explicit SEL instructional activity
2. one literacy session during which instructors read and discussed an SEL-related text with youth
3. an associated SEL literacy extension activity
4. related guiding questions that staff could use to integrate the weekly theme into other OST content.

Most, but not all, OST programs across the six communities created or adopted SEL pacing guides and/or lesson plans. Resources that the OSTIs had developed or external resources like commercially developed pilot lessons for OST programs were crucial. For example, the OSTI in Dallas created its own SEL pacing guide by the third year of PSELI, which it then refined for the fourth year (see the box for details about the structure of this pacing guide). In Palm Beach County, most OST programs began using their partner schools' SEL curriculum (Second Step, created by the nonprofit Committee for Children) to provide lessons to youth. Denver piloted Second Step SEL lesson plans that had been newly designed for OST programs by Committee for Children. Later, Denver's OSTI developed its own SEL curriculum to better fit the needs of the OST programs in its community. However, creating SEL lessons took substantial time, as programs found that they needed to develop a sufficient number of lessons to prevent repetition and to adapt the lessons to different age groups, languages, and OST program content areas.

Stand-Alone SEL Lessons

Invest in acquiring or developing SEL lesson plans and pacing guides that will meet program and youth needs. Do not expect instructors to write their own lesson plans. Initially, the SEL lesson plans and materials offered to the OST programs did not meet all youth needs. For example, OST staff reported that lesson plans were not always appropriate for children of multiple age groups. They also discussed the need for SEL materials in Spanish to better serve their younger bilingual children who were still learning English. In those cases, staff would then have to spend time adapting or creating new lessons. We suggest that OST programs think about what their needs are and then invest in acquiring or developing SEL lesson plans and pacing guides ahead of time so that OST staff are not solely responsible for making these kinds of adaptations or writing their own. There are now at least five programs with SEL content specifically designed for OST settings that programs can access freely or purchase: Second Step, RULER, WINGS, Before the Bullying A.F.T.E.R. School Program, and Girls on the Run (the first two are SEL curricula or instructional tools that can be implemented in any OST setting, and the latter three are OST program models that include SEL; see Jones et al., 2021, for additional information about SEL programs for OST settings or with OST components).[27]

Prepare OST instructors adequately before beginning the delivery of stand-alone SEL lessons. When OST instructors began to deliver stand-alone SEL lessons, some reported that they did not have enough training on how to deliver lessons or were unfamiliar with the use of lesson plans. We suggest delaying the implementation of these types of lessons until adequate training on both SEL and curriculum implementation can occur.

Create dedicated time for SEL. One of the most common challenges that communities encountered in implementing SEL lessons was consistently finding time. Thus, we also recommend creating dedicated time for SEL in OST program schedules. For example, a couple of times a week, OST programs can begin with a 15- to 30-minute "afternoon meeting" when staff can deliver SEL lessons.

Offer repeated opportunities for PD. Staff often mentioned that SEL lesson delivery became easier with practice. Repeated opportunities for PD can strengthen instructor skills in lesson delivery and help instructors who join midyear learn about SEL lesson delivery. For example, some OST programs offered training at the beginning of the school year, as well as before or after winter break.

Some OST Programs Adapted SEL Activities to Fit a Virtual Format in the 2020–2021 School Year

The COVID-19 pandemic also had a profound impact on OST programming during spring 2020 and the 2020–2021 school year, with several OST programs in some communities shifting to offer virtual sessions, while others returned to in-person programming or closed completely. In spring 2021, we observed four fully remote stand-alone OST SEL lessons delivered synchronously to third through fifth graders, and we also asked OST managers in interviews about their virtual SEL offerings during the 2020–2021 school year. Given this small number of observations and interviews, we do not offer tips for success as we do in the other sections. Here we describe how OST programs adjusted their SEL activities to fit in a virtual setting.

SEL Rituals Like Warm Welcomes and Emotion Check-Ins Became the Focus

The use of SEL rituals, such as a five-minute welcome activity to launch a creative writing class, was more common than explicit SEL instruction in virtual OST activities. Rituals included virtual handshakes as a greeting during warm welcome, use of sharing circle prompts as the warm welcome activity (e.g., "How do you feel today?" "Share about one of your favorite games"), or community-building activities, such as a finish-the-story round robin. For emotion check-ins, instructors used pictures or emojis for youth to identify and share their feelings, usually at the start of an activity, or asked youth to identify their emotions through a check-in form prior to logging in to their scheduled activity.

Brain breaks, however, were harder to adapt to virtual settings. Some youth had limited physical space in their homes to participate in movement breaks, and youth lacked interest in video-based brain break activities. OST programs in one community offered options like on-demand one-on-one breakout sessions with a staff member or virtual breakout rooms ("calming rooms") for youth to select as desired. Each of these breakout rooms represented a different mood or feeling (e.g., anxious, frustrated, etc.) and displayed relevant online resources once youth entered the virtual room (e.g., a weblink to view a calming water scene in the anxious room).

OST Programs Reduced Stand-Alone SEL Lessons and Integration

Those that kept stand-alone lessons shortened them. For example, OST programs in one community used shortened SEL lessons that ranged from 15 to 30 minutes total for the week. In addition, most managers eased expectations for SEL integration into other virtual OST activities because of the reduced programming schedule and limited staff experience delivering instruction in a virtual setting.

CHAPTER THREE

Tackling the Challenge of SEL Training for a Fluctuating OST Workforce

Training the OST workforce, particularly direct service instructors who work with young people, is both an essential and challenging component of bringing SEL practices into OST programs. Research consistently shows the importance of PD when it comes to supporting instructors' effective adoption of new concepts or curricula into their practice, with SEL being no exception.[28] This may be especially important for use of written SEL lessons; OST instructors typically do not have prior experience with these.

PD about SEL topics can also reinforce the value of the youth development that OST instructors already do in their day-to-day work with young people. Survey data support this: For all four years of PSELI, more than 90 percent of OST staff agreed on our survey that their SEL PD experiences in a given year aligned with what they already did in their programming.

As important as training the OST workforce in SEL can be, OST programs in all six communities experienced challenges with PD:

- **Frequent staff turnover** was a particularly salient challenge for OST programs. As one OST program manager explained in 2021, "[W]e tend to have a high turnover rate.

So sometimes the staff we start with in the beginning of the year is not always the staff that we end with." As this quote suggests, as OST instructors came and went (sometimes even within a single school year), the SEL training that they received went with them. This left OST programs struggling to train new incoming staff efficiently and effectively.

- **Scheduling conflicts** also posed training challenges. Interviewees explained that because many OST instructors are in school or at another job during the day, it could be difficult to find a training schedule that worked well for everyone. For example, one OST program manager explained in 2021 that the program's instructors were unable to attend SEL trainings scheduled during the school day because their program happened to provide programming during that same time. Scheduling challenges were especially acute for trainings that combined OST instructors from multiple providers or programs, which often occurred throughout PSELI.

- **Low staff attendance** was another barrier to training OST instructors. Attendance challenges were sometimes attributed to scheduling conflicts, but a small number of interviewees explained that a lack of incentive or payment for trainings could also be a factor limiting OST instructor attendance. In addition, some interviewees mentioned that staff perception of the training not being relevant reduced their attendance. This issue of relevance most often applied to joint school-OST trainings that some staff viewed as being classroom-centric and not as focused on SEL in the OST setting, but some OST program staff also felt that the SEL trainings were redundant either with previous trainings or with the practices that they already used in their programs. Regarding trainings on promoting equity in SEL, one OST program manager explained, "[W]e already do a lot of that so it doesn't seem as relevant."

With these challenges (and efforts to mitigate them) in mind, there are several factors to consider when developing an SEL training plan for OST instructors, particularly when it comes to the frequency and timing of training, the training content, and who delivers training to which audiences. SEL trainings varied widely across the six PSELI communities and over the four years of the initiative with respect to each of these factors. We discuss these variations, as well as some common themes that emerged from interview and survey data over time, in the sections that follow.

OST Staff Often Received an Early Kickoff Training That Was Complemented by Additional Trainings Throughout the Year

OST programs across the six communities generally relied on traditional group trainings to develop SEL knowledge and skills in their instructors. However, the total number of training hours in which OST instructors were expected to participate varied widely from community to community and even from year to year. For example, Tacoma dropped the number of expected PD hours from 60 hours in the 2018–2019 school year to 20 hours in the 2019–2020 school year in an effort to reduce the burden on OST staff. Though the total amount of training varied, interview and survey data suggest that, across all six communities, OST instructors generally received SEL training throughout the school year rather than participating in a "one-and-done" model of training. Although OST instructors often received some version of a kickoff training at the start of the year (such as during school preservice days), they typically received additional training at multiple points throughout the school year.

Several communities developed a training plan that incorporated micro-trainings that OST instructors participated in throughout the year, often as part of their regular staff meeting time. For example, Denver developed a series of trainings called SEAL U (Social, Emotional, and Academic Learning University), which consisted of short 30- to 60-minute trainings delivered throughout the school year. Dallas OST program managers met each Monday with their instructors to preview the SEL lessons for that week. During the 2020–2021 school year, Tacoma used 15-minute huddles with OST instructors every program day. The first huddle of every week was dedicated to modeling and discussing that week's SEL activity.

Short micro-training opportunities can help to mitigate both turnover and scheduling challenges. Short trainings more easily fit into OST instructor schedules when they are embedded in existing meetings or if they can be slotted in during brief times of shared availability. For example, Tulsa held "pint-sized" trainings in the morning, when most OST instructors could attend. Although OST programs' shift over time toward more-frequent shorter trainings might have initially been a response to particular barriers, this trend may have had other benefits as well. Shorter, more-frequent trainings can give OST instructors the opportunity to develop skills and knowledge over time, particularly when trainings reinforce or build on each other. The challenge is to deliver these recurring micro-trainings at a time when all staff who need them can participate.

Micro-trainings can also be made available as self-paced virtual training modules, which is what Palm Beach County did in 2020–2021. Not only did they develop a series of eight self-paced training modules on adult SEL, but they also introduced a one-hour self-paced module that focused on getting new instructors up to speed on the basics of SEL. These self-paced trainings were supplemented with live check-in sessions and follow-ups. Short, easily watched videos can be one important tool for OST programs to use to onboard new instructors throughout the school year, reducing the training challenges presented by frequent staff turnover.

SEL Training Content Varied and Evolved

The specific content covered by SEL trainings for OST instructors varied from community to community and, in some cases, even within communities. This level of variation can be a helpful way to differentiate PD by local context, as well as by instructors' diverse needs and interests. Even as content varied, however, we did note some themes in training content across communities, as described in more detail below.

Initial SEL Trainings Typically Focused on Basic "SEL 101" Knowledge

Though training content varied, interview and survey data brought some common themes to the surface. For example, communities typically focused first on imparting foundational SEL knowledge, often called "SEL 101." Our surveys of OST staff suggest that trainings that focused on a basic overview of SEL, and its related definitions, remained a constant over four years: In each of those years, 82 to 89 percent of OST staff reported that their PD focused on SEL 101 information to a moderate-to-great degree. This consistent focus on SEL basics may have been a response to staff turnover; it could also indicate that becoming familiar with, and buying into, foundational SEL knowledge requires persistent time and effort. As the initiative progressed, however, OST staff reported a steadily decreasing need for SEL 101 PD: While more than half (56 percent) of OST staff reported that they needed additional PD on SEL basics in 2018, only a third (34 percent) reported the same by spring 2021.

As time went on, training content evolved to focus increasingly on implementing specific SEL strategies, such as lessons or integrating SEL into OST activities (72 percent of OST staff reported a moderate-to-great degree of focus on implementing specific SEL strategies in 2018, and 87 percent reported this in 2021). For example, OST instructor trainings in Tacoma focused on three specific SEL rituals, and OST instructors in Tulsa received training on implementing the RULER SEL practices.

Offering Differentiated SEL Trainings to OST Instructors Can Have Benefits, But a System for Tracking Participation Must Be in Place

Given the steadily decreasing need for additional PD on SEL 101 training that was reported by OST staff, a beneficial training model could be a two-tracked approach with SEL 101 trainings for new instructors running parallel with a training series with more-advanced SEL topics for returning instructors. Relatedly, some communities offered a menu or suite of PD offerings for OST instructors. For example, Boston After School & Beyond offered more than 20 SEL Circle trainings to OST programs in 2019–2020; OST program staff were required to attend three six-hour weekend sessions and then could select other trainings to attend as desired. Differentiating PD in these ways can help ensure that the trainings in which OST instructors participate match their experience, needs, and interests. However, one challenge inherent in a varied training menu is the need to track which staff members received which trainings. Tracking reduces the risk of repeating trainings that OST instructors already received, lessening the concern that instructors will find trainings redundant and opt out of sessions.

SEL Trainings Placed an Increasing Emphasis on Developing Adult SEL Skills

After an initial focus on training adults to develop SEL skills in young people, several communities focused increasingly on building SEL competencies in adults, such as identifying and managing their own emotions.[d] In spring 2021, 85 percent of OST staff reported that the SEL PD they received focused a moderate-to-great degree on strategies to build their own SEL skills. This was an increase from spring 2018, when 69 percent reported this. One OST SEL director noted in 2019 that their team may have "dropped the ball" by placing more initial focus on SEL instruction than on adult SEL skill-building.

Whether it was a focus from the outset or one that they came to add, interviewees consistently noted that adult SEL skill development was crucial to their efforts. As one interviewee explained in 2021, "It starts with us [adults], and it's all about how we set the tone and how we practice SEL ourselves . . . so focusing on not just your work with students, but what do you change in your practice in order to best serve kids?" In particular, interviewees spoke to the importance of developing adults' skills in relating to other staff and to youth, stress management and emotion regulation, and self-care. Several interviewees also noted that the need to support adults' SEL skills came into even sharper relief as OST program staff navigated the shifting and stressful context of working through the COVID-19 pandemic. Focusing on adult SEL skills comports with research suggesting that the development of adults' own SEL competencies lays the groundwork for then supporting youth SEL.[29]

OST Staff Identified Training on Adapting SEL Practices for Diverse Youth Populations as a Consistent Need

Adapting SEL practices for different youth populations was one area in which OST staff consistently reported needing additional PD. In all four years of survey administration, more than three-quarters of OST staff reported that they needed additional training in strategies to adapt SEL practices for youth with different learning needs. Starting in 2019, the survey included questions about strategies to adapt SEL practices for youth from different linguistic or cultural backgrounds. Here too, more than three-quarters of OST staff consistently reported that they needed additional training, with roughly one-third of staff noting that this was an area of "large need."

---

[d] Some communities placed an emphasis on developing adult SEL skills from the beginning of PSELI. This was the case in Denver. It was also true in Palm Beach County, where—starting in the first year of the initiative—OST program staff participated in a training called "Bringing Yourself to Work" that focused on developing adult SEL skills, such as self-awareness and relationship-building.

OST Staff Wanted More Trainings That Included Modeling and Hands-On Practice

Regardless of content, and across communities, interviewees emphasized that OST staff valued PD that included modeling, opportunities for hands-on practice of SEL skills and lessons, and concrete examples of what SEL should look like during the program. Opportunities for modeling and practice of the SEL rituals and skills that adults were expected to use with young people were often presented as brief training moments during OST staff meetings (e.g., beginning staff meetings with a warm welcome or community circle). This served two purposes in that it gave OST instructors the opportunity to experience firsthand how SEL practices could be enacted in a group setting while also giving them the opportunity to develop the same SEL competencies as the young people they served. These perceived benefits of embedding both modeling and practice in PD opportunities are backed up by a body of PD research that has identified these training features as best practices.[30] As one OST program manager explained in spring 2021,

> modeling those practices for adult social-emotional learning in our meetings has been really good because I think that the best way to learn why something is important is to understand yourself . . . by doing it. . . . We feel better about [our] meetings . . . when we do this, so we should do this for our students.

Trainings with practice and modeling components often came up in interviews as the types of training of which OST staff wanted more.

Many OST Programs Eventually Landed on Providing Some Direct SEL Training to All Staff Plus Additional Training Just for Program Leaders

When it came to both developing and facilitating SEL workshops and trainings, the PSELI communities relied on OSTI leads, coaches, OST program managers and directors, SEL content experts (e.g., curriculum developers), technical assistance partners (e.g., the Weikart Center), and local partner organizations (e.g., other state or local OSTIs, large OST providers). Several communities put together PD schedules that included trainings from a variety of these sources.

The six PSELI communities varied in their approaches to PD and encountered benefits and drawbacks with both a train-the-trainer model (in which OST managers and directors are trained on SEL topics and then expected to pass that knowledge to other OST staff) and a direct training model (in which all OST staff, including instructors, directly participate in SEL training). For example, direct training can help ensure consistency in the quality and amount of training that OST instructors receive, but it also demands a high level of resources. On the other hand, training OST program managers and directors to deliver PD to their staff focuses resources on a part of the OST workforce that experiences less turnover, but there will be inevitable variation in whether and how effectively OST program managers and directors pass their training on to instructors who work directly with youth. In 2018, for example, an OST program manager in a community that employed a train-the-trainer model criticized it for being like a "game of telephone."

One way to mitigate the trade-offs is to employ a hybrid training model in which some trainings are offered to all OST staff and others are provided to leadership staff only. Over the course of PSELI, several communities landed on some version of this hybrid model. For example, in 2017–2018, Dallas relied entirely on a train-the-trainer model in which Big Thought led a variety of SEL trainings with seven site-based SEL program managers who were then expected to share what they learned with the OST instructors at their respective sites. Concerns that this model was limited in its effectiveness and placed significant burden on the SEL program managers prompted a shift: In 2018–2019, OST instructors still received the bulk of their training from SEL program managers but also attended some direct training themselves.

Training a Fluctuating OST Workforce

Plan for staff turnover by creating onboarding materials and easily repeatable SEL training. Though OST programs may not be able to address the challenge of staff turnover itself, they can take steps to minimize turnover's disruption of SEL implementation. Developing clear and concise onboarding materials (e.g., a SEL handbook for new instructors) and designing SEL training that is easily repeatable and accessible for new hires can help ensure that instructors are quickly brought up to speed on SEL in their programs.

Pay for OST instructor time to attend if the PD is outside the regular work schedule. Payment could be included as added hours in staff paychecks or could be distributed as stipends for attendance. Payment for instructor time will not only encourage consistent attendance but can also send an important signal that SEL PD is a priority and that OST instructor time is valued.

Complement longer kickoff trainings with short refresher trainings throughout the year. Kickoff trainings can be a great way to lay a foundation of SEL 101 (e.g., what SEL is, what it should look like in OST instructors' programs, common SEL language) for all OST instructors. Once all instructors are on the same page about current SEL language and expectations, it is important to follow up with regular additional trainings throughout the year. This training progression could be differentiated, such that new instructors receive a series of trainings that reinforce SEL 101 knowledge while more-experienced instructors receive trainings that deepen and expand their existing SEL skills and knowledge.

Consider developing a training model that uses a hybrid delivery approach. Directly training all OST instructors on key elements of SEL can help ensure that high-quality PD is distributed to OST staff who work with young people. However, complementing direct training with additional train-the-trainer opportunities for OST directors and managers can deepen SEL knowledge and skills in those staff members who may stay with the OST program for a longer duration.

Maintain modeling, hands-on practice, and development of adult SEL skills as constants throughout trainings. Interviewees responded positively to trainings and staff meetings that included modeling and opportunities for hands-on practice of SEL rituals and instruction, and they consistently acknowledged the importance of laying an ongoing foundation of adult SEL skills. Building these features into SEL trainings and staff meetings throughout the year can help ensure that OST instructors find their PD opportunities to be engaging, useful, and relevant.

CHAPTER FOUR

Engaging Families to Support Children's SEL

Families and caregivers are central to cultivating children's social and emotional competencies. OST programs can work with families to reinforce children and youth's positive academic, social, and emotional development.[31] Although we did not directly observe family events, we asked OST managers about their family engagement activities during interviews. Here, we draw on these interviews with OST program managers to describe the progression of OST programs' family engagement efforts and the key strategies that they used to engage families in SEL, as well as how managers addressed challenges with outreach.

OST Programs Gradually Broadened Their Efforts to Engage Families in SEL

To further support children's SEL, many OST programs engaged families (including guardians) in their SEL work with the hope that doing so could reinforce SEL for children at home. OST programs' strategies to engage families in SEL evolved over time. During the first and second years of their SEL programming, many managers described general interaction with families at pickup or family events, but they were undecided about how to engage families in SEL specifically. Communication with families about SEL generally started after the SEL program activities themselves became routine, which typically occurred in the second or third year of programming. And although OST managers eventually used multiple formats for outreach, it took some of them time to do so. Initially, most OST managers started by including

SEL content in their family events and then added SEL content to program materials for families or at regular pickup to broaden outreach. A few programs also offered SEL training for families in year four of their SEL programming.

OST Programs Used Three Key Strategies to Engage with Families About SEL

OST program managers who attempted to engage with families about SEL described the following three general strategies.

OST Programs Informed Families About SEL in Materials and Events

OST program managers used family events, visual displays, newsletters, and program calendars as platforms to define SEL and describe their SEL programming to parents and guardians. For example, they used the program calendar or a newsletter to highlight the SEL topic for a given week or month or presented on SEL topics at family events. One manager commented, "There were a lot of parents who came up [at the end of the event] and said they were kind of grateful to understand it because they'd been hearing a lot of, 'We're in this SEL [program], we do Second Step,' but they didn't really understand the level of significance of it." Some managers also used the family events and visual displays to showcase youth work and SEL projects. OST programs in Dallas used a new app messaging system for families called Remind to provide information about the weekly SEL focus, resources related to the SEL focus (e.g., lists of websites and books), and an optional question of the week or family polls to encourage family discussions.

OST Staff Included Families in SEL Rituals

Several OST programs used regular in-person opportunities to connect with families, such as including a warm welcome (e.g., greeting parents by name), posting a family joke of the day, or having families select how staff should greet them at pickup time (e.g., a handshake or joke). One program had a daily optimistic closure routine for youth that ran during the last 20 minutes of programming; families could observe this routine, and youth greeted their own families with a warm welcome upon arrival. A few programs had a quick SEL reflection activity available for parents or guardians at pickup, such as writing an encouraging message or their hopes for youth and then posting these on a bulletin board. Managers also described using a warm welcome and optimistic closure at their family events and other face-to-face gatherings, even if these were virtual meetups. In addition, a few programs provided families with conversation starters like "Would you rather . . . ?" or "What was the best part of your day?" at pickup to encourage a warm welcome between families and their children.

Programs Provided Families with SEL Activities and Strategies to Use with Their Children

The third way in which OST program staff engaged families was by providing them with specific SEL activities and strategies to use with their children. For example, some managers described organizing take-home activities to encourage relationship-building, such as a family tree project (which required that youth talk with their families to complete it), weekend scavenger hunt assignments related to the SEL theme, dinner conversation prompts, SEL-themed bingo, or event prizes designed to encourage shared family experiences (such as a gingerbread house kit or treats for a family movie night). In Denver, families received SEL-themed books to read with their children at home; each book related to the SEL topics covered in the program. Some OST programs organized similar relationship-building activities that took place at their family events, such as a family story-writing activity or building a birdhouse.

A few programs also provided formal training or guidance for parents and guardians on general SEL topics and strategies for home activities. For example, some programs in Palm Beach County offered family training sessions on stress management in the home and building emotional safety. Similarly, some programs in Denver held monthly sessions for families to discuss SEL topics like empathy. Other OST programs engaged families in guided-SEL activities, such as a "paint your values" family night at which staff led a group discussion on values (e.g., "What is a value?" "What are your family values?"), and families then co-created a painting representing their family values. Another OST program organized an event for youth and their families at which they could co-create glitter jars that they could shake and watch as a calming or mindful brain break activity. In some

cases, youth led this activity. Through this joint endeavor, families learned what brain breaks are and why they are important.

Engaging Families in SEL Took Time, Advance Planning, and In-Person Contact

Across communities, it became clear that planning was essential to engaging families effectively in SEL. First, it took time for managers to figure out how to implement SEL programming for youth and for staff to grow in their own SEL knowledge and practice before they then communicated about it with families. For example, a program manager new to the position commented, "The parents, they welcome these [family] events. They're eager for more. [But] it has been challenging [because] many times I don't feel comfortable to do those brain breaks and SEL mindfulness exercises [with parents]. . . . I feel like I'm a fish swimming out of the water." It also took time for OST managers to plan how to engage families, what SEL content or activities to include in family events or newsletters, and which strategies would encourage attendance or participation and then to budget for events and incentives.

But once the in-person SEL activities with families were done, managers often described them as well-received. One manager noted, "The families that were at the event really did talk about [their values] and represented [them] in their pictures, and they really enjoyed that conversation together." Another commented, "I think what has been working well is my staff really engage in conversations with parents, and having the parents engage in the optimistic closure, because then those parents know what their students are working on throughout the week. But what I think could be better is finding a way to make sure the parents are reading the newsletter, and I haven't really brainstormed [how] to do that yet." While passive communication methods like emails, take-home activities, and newsletters allowed for broad outreach, it was hard for managers to gauge whether families read them. To encourage participation, one manager sent take-home SEL activities and provided an incentive for youth who completed and returned them.

Managers also cited challenges related to connecting with families that were not specific to SEL. For example, several noted challenges with getting families to attend events because of such barriers as lack of transportation, conflicts with work schedules, or events occurring during dinnertime. Multiple managers reported that providing food and prizes encouraged attendance: "What's been communicated from our families is that both parents have to work. So us offering [family events] later, and providing dinner, is an incentive." Another commented on the importance of direct, personalized outreach to improve attendance: "It's not just a piece of paper. We are definitely communicating with families on the importance of being there, and why they should be there, and how they can celebrate their student by being there." A few program managers also reported language barriers; some parents or guardians were unable to understand event presentations or written materials. To address this challenge, some programs translated materials or designated a staff member to communicate with families in their preferred language.

Finally, a handful of managers commented on SEL-specific challenges in communicating with families. These had to do with cultural differences or differing perceptions of SEL. A few managers explained that discussion of emotions was a challenging practice to encourage in the home because some of their families came from cultures in which emotions are not openly discussed. One manager also highlighted that SEL can put parents and guardians on the defensive because it makes them feel like "[the] practices I have in place as a parent are not the right ones." To address this misunderstanding, the manager focused on giving brief introductions to SEL competencies at family nights and provided SEL-themed take-home activities instead of offering a primer on SEL strategies.

TIPS FOR SUCCESS
Engaging Families in SEL

Set aside time to plan outreach efforts with families, including non–English-speaking families. Consider how to engage families, what SEL content or activities to include, or translation needs to reach non–English-speaking families. Also consider a budget for SEL events or activity materials, as well as food or other incentives (e.g., dinner, snacks, prizes) to encourage attendance at in-person events or participation in take-home SEL activities.

Offer multiple methods to connect families to SEL, including a program calendar, email, newsletters, or a bulletin board (e.g., to highlight SEL activities, monthly or weekly SEL topics, youth SEL projects, or online SEL resources), and in-person contact to broaden outreach and distribution of SEL resources for families to further support their children's SEL at home.

Provide families with specific SEL activities to encourage their children's SEL. Directors commented that families were not always aware of SEL but that families were generally receptive and participated when offered SEL-themed activities or practices, such as the conversation starters to greet their children at pickup or family relationship-building activities (e.g., family story assignment, games).

Use regular in-person opportunities to highlight SEL content and practices, such as modeling use of SEL rituals with families, explaining a take-home SEL activity, or spotlighting youth SEL projects during daily pickup.

CHAPTER FIVE

Improving Program Quality to Advance SEL Activities

Having a continuous quality improvement (CQI) cycle was an important way for OST programs to assess how SEL activities were being delivered to youth and where they might need to adjust. The OST programs in PSELI came from different starting points in terms of experience with CQI; some were seasoned experts, while others were brand new.

Over Time, a Common Five-Step CQI Process Took Hold Across the OST Programs

CQI processes are quite common in quality improvement work and were used by the technical assistance providers who worked across the PSELI communities, as well as by the OSTIs who supported CQI work in the OST programs. As a first step, OST programs set up a timeline for data-use cycles, which provided a structure for the CQI process. The timeline established when the remaining four steps (data collection, data analysis, action planning, and SEL committee meetings to monitor progress toward meeting goals) would occur and who would complete them. These cycles ranged from every one-and-a-half months to twice a year and often revolved around observations of programming by external partners. For example, in Denver, a quality improvement coach from the OSTI conducted an observation of the program, debriefed the program on its scores and ways to improve, and then returned to observe again at the start of another cycle.

The second step was data collection. Once the OST programs determined which type of data to collect (e.g., observations of programming, staff surveys, youth surveys, administrative records), actual collection of that data occurred at least twice a year or sometimes daily, depending on the type of data. Program observations were typically conducted by either the OSTI or a technical assistance partner, while staff and youth surveys were distributed by the OST program alone or jointly with their evaluation partner who provided the data collection platform.

The third step, data analysis, was a multistep process. A data staff member at the OST program or the OSTI analyzed the data and generated usable metrics or reports for use by the OST program's SEL committee. If data came from multiple sources, such as observation data from the OSTI and internal staff survey data, a designated OST staff member served as the point person for compiling the multiple data sources. As one OST manager described, "Once they give [the observation data] back to us, we meet with our team and see where we scored low and use those data to make our improvement goals. If we are high in an area, that tells us what we are doing well [and should continue]."

As a fourth step, OST programs created action plans that made program improvement concrete, outlining specific goals and the actual steps involved in improvement. For many of the OST programs already familiar with quality improvement for general positive youth development practices, these action plans provided an opportunity to focus their existing CQI processes on specific SEL goals. For example, in Boston, the OSTI guided programs in creating site-level growth plans, which were used to identify goals and monitor progress in three areas: program structure (e.g., arrival logistics, activity transitions), a specific SEL practice of focus (e.g., warm welcomes, optimistic closures), and data use. At the close of the school year, OST managers received a diagnostic report, which provided a snapshot end-of-the-year rating and brief narrative completed by the OSTI coach for each of the areas in the program's action plan. This corresponded with an increase in the frequency of data use and OST staff confidence using data that year.

FIGURE 5.1
OST Programs' Five-Step CQI Process

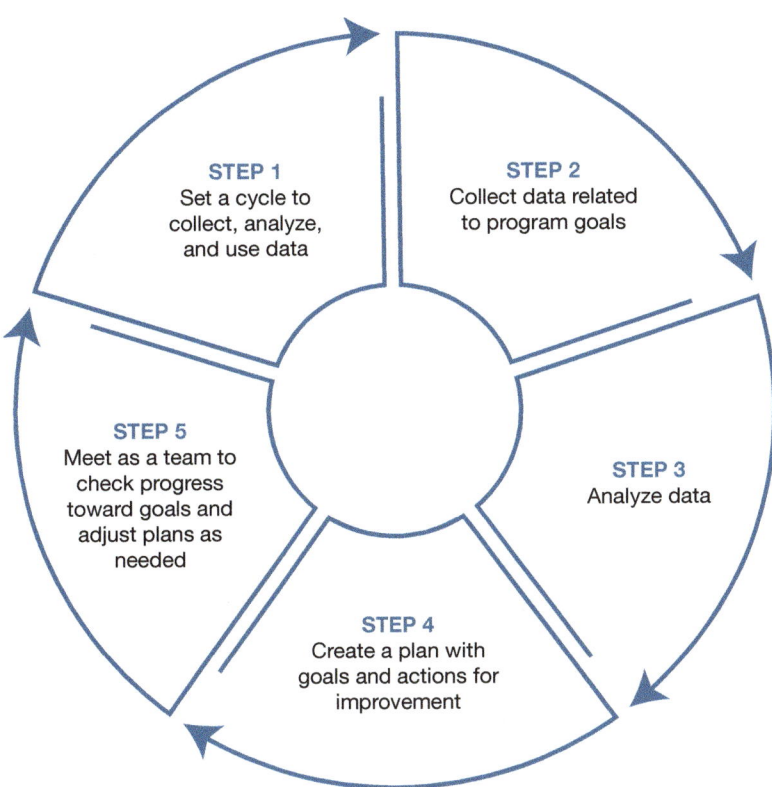

STEP 1
Set a cycle to
collect, analyze,
and use data

STEP 2
Collect data related
to program goals

STEP 3
Analyze data

STEP 4
Create a plan with
goals and actions for
improvement

STEP 5
Meet as a team to
check progress
toward goals and
adjust plans as
needed

As a final step, OST programs held SEL committee meetings. These provided accountability for the CQI processes and checks on the progress toward goals outlined in the action plans. The meetings typically occurred on site, monthly, and at times convenient for program staff to attend and included the OST program manager, select OST program staff (e.g., assistant or activities director), and sometimes a data coach from the OSTI. These meetings were an opportunity to discuss implementation challenges and successes and adjust plans as needed after reviewing the most current data. Figure 5.1 illustrates this five-step process.

For example, the OSTI leaders in Boston described how the five components of this process can work to drive SEL improvement. At the start of the school year, OST programs established their program practice goals, such as using welcoming rituals and optimistic closures at the start and end of activities. OSTI leaders and SEL coaches identified tools to measure these outcomes and reviewed these with the OST program manager. Leaders from the OSTI and OST program jointly established the data-use cycle timeline, establishing which data to collect, how often, and by whom, along with the timeline for analysis and action planning (Step 1). An SEL coach observed an OST program (Step 2) in the fall using the National Institute on Out-of-School Time's (NIOST's) Assessment of Program Practices Tool (APT). At least one staff member from each OST program trained to become a certified observer with this tool, which equipped them with knowledge of best practices assessed by the tool and the rationale behind the tool's ratings that they could then apply when creating a quality improvement plan. Upon completion of data analysis by NIOST and the OSTI (Step 3), the coach provided a diagnostic report to the OST program that outlined whether the program met benchmarks for implementing practices that build children's development of social-emotional skills "most of the time." The coach met with the OST program manager to review the report and highlighted areas of practice in which the program met the benchmark to ensure that those practices continued. From the practices for which the program did not meet the benchmark, the coach and OST program staff chose one for which to develop an action plan for improvement (Step 4). One program scored low in implementing reflective practices at the end of activities and created an action plan for improvement in that area. The action plan included training staff on reflective practices, including how these practices help to reinforce learning and build relationships, and practical strategies for embedding reflective practices or closing circles into program activities. The coach then attended the monthly SEL committee meetings (Step 5) held by the OST program to provide support in monitoring progress toward meeting their goal and provided coaching to staff while on site. The data collection cycle repeated in the spring with another observation by the coach, after which the program's SEL committee reviewed data with the coach to gauge progress toward meeting the benchmarks.

Different Types of Data Informed Programs' Multifaceted Improvement Goals

Table 5.1 summarizes the types of data collected by the OSTIs and OST programs in PSELI, the types of tools used to collect the data, and the purpose of those data as reported by OST program managers. For example, to inform goal-setting and monitor implementation, OST programs tended to rely on formal program

TABLE 5.1

Data Collected by OSTIs and OST Programs in PSELI

Purpose of Data	Types of Data Collected	Tools Used[a]
Determine amount of services that youth receive	• Enrollment • Attendance • Demographics	• Management information systems (e.g., Salesforce, Cityspan)
Inform goal-setting	• Program quality observations • Youth surveys of program experience or quality • Youth surveys of their own social-emotional skills • Staff surveys of youth social-emotional skills	• APT, SEL PQA, AQuA/6 Dimensions of Quality Teaching and Learning • Survey of Academic and Youth Outcomes for Youth • Holistic Student Assessment • Survey of Academic and Youth Outcomes for Teachers, Devereux Student Strengths Assessment, Staff Rating of Youth Behavior
Monitor implementation	• Program quality observations • Youth surveys of program experience or quality • Youth surveys of their own social-emotional skills • Staff surveys of youth social-emotional skills	• APT, SEL PQA, AQuA/6 Dimensions of Quality Teaching and Learning • Survey of Academic and Youth Outcomes for Youth • Holistic Student Assessment • Survey of Academic and Youth Outcomes for Teachers, Devereux Student Strengths Assessment
Improve program satisfaction	• Staff surveys of program experience or quality • Family surveys of program experience or quality	• Developed in house by individual OST programs
Identify SEL best practices, provide feedback	• Informal program observations focused on SEL implementation	• Walkthrough tools developed by OSTIs and technical assistance providers

[a] NIOST[32] provides a suite of evaluation tools, which includes APT, the Survey of Academic and Youth Outcomes for Youth, and the Survey of Academic and Youth Outcomes for Teachers; the Weikart Center[33] provides the SEL PQA and Staff Rating of Youth Behavior; Partnerships in Education and Resilience[34] provides the Holistic Student Assessment; Aperture Education[35] provides the Devereux Student Strengths Assessment; and Dallas Afterschool[36] provides the Afterschool Quality Advancement (AQuA) and 6 Dimensions of Quality Teaching and Learning tools.

NOTE: SEL PQA = Social and Emotional Learning Program Quality Assessment.

observations—conducted by external coaches or technical assistance providers using validated tools like the Weikart Center's SEL PQA, developed from 2016 to 2018—and surveys of youth's social-emotional skills. To identify best practices and provide feedback to staff to inform change in program practice, OST programs with access to such a tool generally used SEL-specific walkthrough observations, which were often conducted by the OST manager and tailored to the specific SEL approach of that community. Data collection methods varied because some types of data were more appropriately collected using surveys (e.g., youth or family perceptions of program offerings), while some were better gauged through observations (e.g., assessments of program practices).

Not all OST programs collected all the types of data listed in Table 5.1. In fact, for many OST programs, too much data became overwhelming and unusable. On the other hand, too little data made it difficult to set goals for quality improvement. OST program managers described these challenges with the data they were collecting on their own, separate from the data collected for the research study. Finding the right balance of how much and which data to collect to best meet program improvement goals is not unique to the PSELI programs. Prior research on data use in the OST setting suggests several helpful strategies to make CQI more accessible, including setting explicit goals for data collection and use and creating an inventory of data to be used that includes which questions each piece of data helps answer.[37] Each OST program in PSELI received support in its CQI work from its OSTI and external technical assistance providers, who had expertise in collecting, analyzing, and interpreting data.

Different types of data can be more relevant to specific staff roles within an OST program. The most common type of data collected among the PSELI programs was enrollment and attendance. These data were used to answer the question of who was being served by the program to inform revised recruitment and retention strategies. OST managers also commonly cited using observation data on the quality of SEL program practices to drive their improvement processes. An OST manager noted the importance of observation data by saying, "The predictable cadence of walkthroughs and data collection and feedback [that we had with the SEL PQA] really helped with our overall quality." For example, when one OST program scored low in youth voice on its external observation assessment, the program started being intentional about instructing staff that certain activities were to be youth-led, with staff acting as facilitators, and provided training to staff to meet that goal. Ensuring that different staff within an OST program have data tied to their specific roles can help distribute the work of quality improvement among the staff.

TIPS FOR SUCCESS

Improving Program Quality

Start with a narrow set of data closely related to the OST program's SEL goals. Too much data can become unusable, whereas too little data can make it difficult to pinpoint areas for improvement. Clearly defining SEL goals and collecting data related to those goals can help keep the scope of CQI more manageable. For example, if a goal is to develop youth leadership, collect one or two data elements that clearly relate to that goal—e.g., a survey question for youth about their perception of having a say in OST program activities or the rate of participation in a youth advisory committee. OST programs should focus on collecting data that are actionable, meaning that they lend themselves to specific steps toward program improvement.

Establish processes, such as data use cycles and action plans, to support data analysis and use. Cycles for data collection, analysis, interpretation, and use provide a structure for CQI, and action plans can create accountability for the actual work of program improvement. Regular meetings to review data and progress toward SEL goals can further ensure that CQI work is on track.

Hire or contract with a dedicated staff member with data expertise and the requisite time to manage the collection, analysis, and use of data that robust CQI requires. For OST programs with smaller numbers of staff, partnering with an external organization or OSTI to conduct some or all of the CQI work can allow staff to focus on managing programming for young people without sacrificing CQI work and program improvement.

CHAPTER SIX

Ways OSTIs Can Support SEL in OST Programs

Incorporating high-quality SEL into OST programming might feel like a daunting task for OST providers. Each layer of SEL implementation—identifying SEL practices and/or lessons to implement, training and supporting staff, and monitoring implementation, all while engaging families along the way—takes time, capacity, and resources that individual OST programs might lack. Therefore, external organizations like an OSTI can play an essential role in supporting OST program efforts to implement high-quality SEL instruction. See the first section of this report for additional information about what OSTIs are and the role they played in PSELI.

The following sections articulate the different functions that external organizations (whether an OSTI, a technical assistance provider, or a mayor's office) can provide to OST programs. We describe how the six communities' OSTIs provided support to individual OST programs, and we provide tips on ways in which external organizations can support OST programs' SEL efforts.

OSTIs Bolstered the Internal Capacity of OST Programs by Connecting Them to Broader Networks of Support

Where a stand-alone OST program might not have the resources, influence, or staffing to drive its SEL work, an OSTI can step in and connect that program to a broader network of support. In PSELI, OSTIs typically did this via one or more of three strategies:

(1) providing OSTI staff to support SEL implementation in OST programs, (2) learning from experts in the field of SEL and sharing that expertise with OST programs, and (3) garnering funding for SEL in OST programs. We discuss each of these three strategies in the paragraphs that follow.

OSTIs in several communities hired new SEL staff or shifted current staff's assignments to focus specifically on SEL. These new or reassigned staff typically

- provided SEL PD support to OST staff

- facilitated professional learning communities to enable the OST program managers to meet and share information

- managed school-OST partnerships and coordination

- helped determine an overall SEL strategy for OST programs, including selecting which SEL resources to use.

OSTIs in all six communities also interfaced with expert technical assistance providers in the field of SEL at some point over the course of four years, gaining expertise that they could then share with OST programs. Like the OST programs themselves, OSTIs might not have SEL expertise available in house. While OST programs can, of course, reach out to SEL experts directly themselves, an OSTI can create efficiencies by receiving technical assistance and then disseminating that information throughout its network of OST programs.

The six OSTIs worked with a range of technical assistance organizations, some national and some local. Most consistently, OSTIs worked with CASEL and the Weikart Center to gain SEL or broader program quality expertise. Support varied by community, but CASEL and the Weikart Center generally supported OSTI staff by helping with developing a strategic plan or vision for SEL in OST, strategizing for continuous improvement, providing PD through trainings or by supporting the work of SEL coaches, and helping to develop instructional or quality improvement resources to support SEL implementation in OST programs. The knowledge, skills, tools, and perspectives that technical assistance providers brought to the OSTI could then be shared with OST programs to inform SEL implementation on the ground.

Finally, OSTIs garnered funding that supported OST programs' SEL work. SEL instructional resources and PD cost money, and OST programs may not have the resources to purchase or pay for what they need to effectively implement SEL in their programs. They also may not have the bandwidth to add SEL fundraising to their scope of work. When this is the case, OSTIs and other external partners can advocate on behalf of OST programs to their local and state government and to philanthropies to seek private or public monies to support their SEL work.

OSTIs Identified or Developed SEL Instructional Content for OST Programs

Historically, SEL instructional content designed specifically for the OST context has been limited, as we have described above. Therefore, OSTIs across the six communities played a significant role in first helping to set a vision for what SEL could look like in OST programming and then, in some cases, developing SEL instructional materials to support that vision.

An early focus for OSTIs was to create a shared definition of SEL for their communities and what it should look like in the OST space. Some OSTIs did this by helping to adapt or develop an SEL framework, which is a document that names and organizes SEL competencies to help OST staff understand and communicate about them and help youth build them. OSTIs were in a good position to take this work on because of their connections with SEL experts and school districts and because they could communicate a shared SEL vision across multiple OST programs. For example, in the 2017–2018 school year, Boston After School & Beyond (in collaboration with Boston Public Schools) developed a document called "Portrait of a Social and Emotional Learner" to guide sites' SEL work. In Tacoma, the OSTI helped to create a glossary of shared SEL terms and definitions (e.g., "SEL explicit instruction") to help develop a common language that both school and OST staff could use.

Over the course of several years, five of the six OSTIs developed sequenced SEL lessons or short activities for direct service OST instructors to use. In Dallas, Big Thought consulted with Dallas Afterschool (another local OSTI) to create an SEL scope and sequence for OST programs. They coordinated their activities with the school-day SEL curriculum (Harmony SEL) and focused on activities—such as reading specific books that they provided to each OST program and asking prewritten discussion questions—that a wide variety of OST program providers could use. The Opportunity Project in Tulsa created, with the school district, an SEL toolkit for staff that included a playbook on three SEL signature practices, SEL self-reflection questions, and an SEL activity jar that contained conversation prompts related to feelings, including productive ways to manage anger. The Opportunity Project also developed an optional pacing guide template, a lesson plan template, and an SEL weekly plan dry erase board to help OST programs incorporate SEL into their programming. And in Tacoma, the Greater Tacoma Community Foundation developed its own 15-minute SEL lessons (called SEL spotlights) for OST instructors to implement in their programs. The SEL spotlights were based on weekly SEL themes like "Getting to Know Me" and "Being a Friend."

Several SEL curricula and programs have become available for OST settings since 2020. As noted in a previous section, The Wallace Foundation sponsored OST-specific instructional materials for Second Step and RULER (both well-established SEL curricula designed for the school day). Therefore, rather than developing new content, part of an OSTI's role could be identifying *existing* SEL instructional content, reviewing materials to gauge their appropriateness for the OST programs in the OSTI's community, adapting or adding to them, and then training OST programs in their use.

OSTIs Developed and Provided Professional Development About SEL for OST Staff

Over the course of four years, OSTIs in every community played a key role in developing and facilitating PD opportunities that helped build OST program staff's SEL knowledge and skills. OSTIs did this through the SEL trainings described in an earlier section of this report, with OSTI staff often taking the lead in designing the SEL training plan, as well as delivering the training.

OSTIs also often took responsibility for providing OST program staff—particularly leadership staff—with SEL coaching and opportunities for cross-site collaboration. The OSTI SEL coaches performed a variety of functions, including helping OST program staff build SEL skills, designing SEL-related instructional content, observing instruction, giving feedback to OST program staff, modeling SEL instruction, supporting SEL data use, and leading

SEL training. In several communities, coaches also played a role in building relationships between OST program and school staff; ensuring that their SEL practices were consistent and mutually reinforcing; managing program logistics; monitoring and advising on program quality broadly; or serving as a bridge between OSTIs, school districts, and sites.[e]

As with the trainings, coaching models included direct SEL-focused coaching of OST instructors and/or "coaching the coaches." Palm Beach County implemented an example of a hybrid SEL coaching model that combined the two strategies. In this community, an SEL coach who worked for the OSTI delivered coaching at least once a month to OST instructors. During these visits, the coach would typically meet with the site OST manager to discuss areas of need, deliver a short PD session to OST program staff, observe a program session and provide one-on-one feedback to the observed instructor, and then meet again with the program manager to discuss next steps. SEL coaching and peer mentoring at the OST managers' level supplemented direct coaching of OST instructors.

Over four years of staff surveys, a majority (74 percent or higher) of OST staff reported receiving some amount of coaching or mentoring on SEL topics, though this varied by community. There was also an increase in the frequency of coaching on SEL topics over the course of four years: By 2021, about one-third of OST program staff reported receiving monthly coaching, and one-fifth reported receiving coaching on at least a weekly basis, compared with 2018, when a majority of program staff (68 percent) reported receiving coaching only one to six times a year.

OSTIs experienced some challenges in coordinating coaching across multiple OST programs, with some interviewees describing inconsistency in the frequency and amount of coaching provided to different programs. Sometimes this variation was intentional and responsive to the different levels of support needed by different programs or individuals, but sometimes it reflected a lack of organization or clarity about how coaching would be enacted on the ground. In spite of these challenges, OST program staff at

---

[e] Developing the partnerships between OSTIs and school districts and between OST programs and schools was a key component of PSELI. Although this report is focused on SEL in OST programs specifically, partnership development is covered in detail in prior RAND reports on PSELI, such as the case study reports that we link to in Chapter 7 of this report and the 2020 report *Early Lessons from Schools and Out-of-School Time Programs Implementing Social and Emotional Learning* (www.rand. org/t/RRA379-1).

all levels expressed appreciation for the coaching that they did receive. They acknowledged the knowledge and expertise that coaches brought to the table and appreciated coaches' responsiveness and willingness to tailor coaching to meet staff needs. In interviews, program staff often cited more coaching or more in-depth coaching as a desired support.

In addition to coaching supports, OSTIs also hosted meetings to bring together OST program managers from across the community. Among other program-related topics, these meetings provided opportunities for developing SEL skills and knowledge, coordinating and monitoring SEL implementation, and collaborating and sharing best practices across programs. These meetings, which could be considered professional learning communities, were highly valued by OST program leadership. However, as with trainings, it could be difficult to find times when staff from different OST programs could meet with one another, particularly given the varying and part-time schedules that staff frequently navigate.

OSTIs Led CQI Processes for SEL in OST Programs

Robust CQI entails more than just collecting data. It requires a comprehensive data use system that includes the people, processes, and technology necessary to analyze and make decisions using data.[38] OSTIs can be well positioned to provide such a data system to support the SEL work of OST programs.

OSTIs can buttress OST program capacity by providing staff with expertise in data use, SEL coaches, and contracts with external technical assistance providers to either directly conduct or support CQI activities at OST programs. OSTIs might also have the capacity—in the form of either qualified in-house staff or partnerships with experts in the field—to develop new SEL-specific measurement tools. For example, in two communities, the OSTIs and technical assistance providers partnered to create SEL walkthrough tools to monitor program implementation and provide feedback to staff on their SEL instructional practices. In one community, these walkthrough observations occurred three times per year, and OST program managers reported using feedback from those walkthroughs to make changes, such as ensuring that all staff used warm welcomes.

In terms of technology, OSTIs can provide management information systems to collect, store, and access data. Acquiring, using, and maintaining these systems can be cost- and time-prohibitive for individual OST programs. In Tacoma, the OSTI (in partnership with the school district) spent multiple years investing in and developing an online registration tool and data dashboard that incorporated school district data, such as data about school attendance and youth demographics, for use by OST programs. This can be an important source of data for OSTIs to understand which populations are being served by OST programs and what gaps in services exist. Because the online registration tool and data dashboard were housed within the school district, data-sharing involved negotiations between the OSTI and the district regarding who owned which data, who could store it, and who could access it. Tacoma's experience highlights the importance of having an external organization that can tackle data-related challenges on behalf of OST programs. In Boston and Palm Beach County, the long-standing OSTIs used their existing management information systems to allow programs to track and retrieve their data. The systems included data visualizations and data dashboards that aided OST programs in identifying areas of strengths and areas for improvement. Proper procedures for consent, data safeguarding, and data deidentification were put into place when sharing data between organizations.

OSTIs can offer data use processes to aid OST programs in setting data-based goals to inform SEL quality improvement. Chief among these is coaching. In all PSELI communities, coaches engaged in many, if not all, of the following CQI activities: conducting observations, guiding OST program managers through data interpretation, building data literacy, identifying goals based on data, facilitating action planning, and monitoring progress toward program improvement. OSTIs can also develop and provide oversight for processes led by OST programs, like action planning and SEL implementation meetings.

Finally, OSTIs can modify programs' existing CQI processes to have a more explicit SEL focus. For example, the OSTI in Palm Beach County enhanced the focus on SEL in its well-established CQI process. To focus on SEL program improvement, the OSTI developed an observation rubric to address areas similar to those identified in the CASEL Schoolwide SEL Walkthrough rubric[39] (e.g., adult SEL practice, SEL framework and explicit SEL instruction, SEL practice integration, and parent engagement). The observation rubric corresponded to PD topics, and the SEL coach used it to identify areas of support for the OST programs. In Boston, the OSTI developed a new coaching model in which external coaches used a diagnostic process toolkit and growth plan. This ensured that the coaches' work was in keeping with the OSTI's approach to SEL implementation. These OSTIs' adjustments to their CQI processes corresponded with increased reports by OST program managers of engaging in SEL-related CQI. Across all communities, clearly linking CQI processes to programs' SEL goals made it easier for OST program managers to use the data to plan for improvement.

Ways OSTIs Can Support SEL in OST Programs

Articulate the relationship between the OSTI and the OST programs in its system to determine the areas in which OSTI support may be appropriate and valuable. The role that an OSTI could best play in supporting SEL implementation will vary depending on local context and the nature of the existing relationships between an OSTI and the programs in its system. Therefore, OSTIs should work with OST programs to define those OSTI-OST relationships (and make explicit the expectations and assumptions at play within those relationships) as a critical first step in supporting programs' SEL work.

Identify specific gaps in OST program capacity that an OSTI and its partners (e.g., content experts, school district) could fill. The goal is not for OSTIs to recreate (or compete with) work that is already being done on the ground in OST programs but to ask what they can do to support programs' ongoing SEL work. The answer to that question is a great starting point for determining where to focus OSTI attention and support.

Determine SEL instructional content needs. Once OST program needs concerning SEL instructional content have been articulated, OSTIs might be well-positioned to do the heavy lifting related to searching for existing resources that will meet those needs. If resources exist but need adaptation, or if entirely new content needs to be developed, OSTIs might have the capacity to develop content themselves as appropriate or could work with SEL content experts to do so.

Work closely with OST programs to develop an SEL PD plan that fits OST staff needs and schedules. If they have the capacity, OSTIs can develop PD opportunities for SEL. However, OSTIs should not be developing a blueprint for SEL PD in a vacuum. Instead, OSTIs can collaborate with programs to ensure that PD opportunities are relevant, nonredundant, and held on days and times that work for program staff. If developing PD opportunities, OSTIs should consider including coaching and professional learning communities along with trainings in their schedules of professional supports for program staff.

Offer OST programs processes and resources to make CQI accessible, focused, and actionable. Whether in the form of technology supports, data collection, data analysis, or provision of SEL-focused data collection tools, OSTIs might have the capacity to provide supports that make CQI more attainable for OST programs. OSTIs may be able to leverage their resources to address gaps or constraints in OST programs' CQI systems.

CHAPTER SEVEN

Recommendations to Support SEL-Focused OST Programming

In this report, we summarized what afterschool OST programs and OSTIs from six communities did in a SEL initiative to support children's social and emotional development. Based on our analysis of their work, we offer the following recommendations for OST programs and OSTI leaders who wish to offer SEL programming to youth.

While there are many ways to approach SEL instruction in OST programming, we suggest that those new to SEL work take a phased approach to deepen their efforts as staff build their knowledge of SEL skills and practices (e.g., providing staff training before adding SEL integration). Additionally, there are many ways that OSTIs or similar organizations can support OST programs in providing SEL programming, and we offer recommendations for OSTIs as well.

Finally, we note that we plan to publish a how-to guide with sample artifacts and resources to outline in more detail some of these steps for incorporating SEL content and practices into OST programming.

Infusing SEL Practices into Programming for Youth

Infusing SEL into programming for children and youth can take the form of short SEL rituals, integrating SEL

Suggested Reading for OST Programs Working with School Partners on SEL

We encourage readers, especially those working with school partners on SEL, to reference our in-depth SEL case studies that spotlight how school and OST program partnerships approached common challenges with SEL implementation, such as finding time for SEL and building adult SEL skills, among others. We also have a cross-cutting report that briefly summarizes each of these case studies and highlights shared themes among them. This overview report, *Strengthening Students' Social and Emotional Skills: Lessons from Six Case Studies of Schools and Out-of-School-Time Program Partners*, is available at wallacefoundation.org and rand.org/pseli and includes links to the six individual case studies for quick reference.

content or instructional strategies into existing activities, and providing direct stand-alone lessons on SEL topics. OST program leaders (and their OSTIs) can take the following actions:

1. **Communicate clear expectations to OST instructors about the SEL practices to use with youth.**

   a. Tell OST instructors if they are expected to use SEL rituals, integrate SEL, and/or use a written lesson plan.

2. **Start by using SEL rituals before phasing in SEL instruction.**

   a. Provide training to all OST program staff (and volunteers) on the use of short SEL rituals. The training should include time for modeling the rituals and then for staff to practice them. Training should also include examples of how to adapt rituals to different contexts (e.g., snack versus homework block, use with younger versus older children).

   b. Use regular staff meetings as an opportunity to model use of SEL rituals and encourage adult practice.

   c. Provide OST instructors with specific written options, prompts, and activities for SEL rituals, such as sharing circles or welcoming activities.

3. **Next, support OST instructors in integrating SEL into regular program activities, such as art or sports.**

   a. Provide OST instructors with training that includes modeling, specific examples, and several opportunities for them to practice.

   b. Designate planning time for OST instructors to discuss or write down how they will integrate SEL content into their planned activities.

4. **If including stand-alone SEL lessons, take time to prepare for OST instructor delivery.**

   a. Develop the SEL content directly, modify existing content, or adopt without modification newer SEL resources specifically designed for OST settings to meet program and youth needs.

b. Provide written SEL lesson plans to OST instructors instead of expecting instructors to create their own.

c. Train OST instructors on how to use lesson plans and deliver stand-alone lessons, including repeated opportunities for practice during meetings or trainings throughout the year.

d. Designate time in the master schedule for the stand-alone SEL lessons.

Approaching SEL Training for a Fluctuating OST Workforce

Staff require ongoing training opportunities to build their knowledge of SEL and their skill in integrating and teaching SEL. OST program leaders (and their OSTIs) can take the following actions:

1. **Deliver multiple PD opportunities spread throughout the year.**

   a. Start with longer kickoff SEL trainings at the beginning of the school year, followed by short micro-training sessions delivered throughout the year.

   b. Create onboarding packages for new staff to quickly orient them to SEL and specific SEL programming and schedule time for new staff to consume that information; this minimizes the disruption caused by staff turnover.

   c. Train OST staff on the basics of SEL first, followed by continuous opportunities for development of adult SEL skills.

   d. Provide staff with training on adult SEL skills to help them develop their own practice, such as relating to other staff and to youth, stress management and emotion regulation, and self-care.

   e. Include training for OST instructors on how to adapt SEL instruction and practices for different youth populations (e.g., by age, by lived experiences); staff consistently reported a need for this support.

   f. Differentiate training for new and experienced staff to deepen staff practice and reduce redundant training.

2. **Provide support to encourage trainee attendance, including ongoing opportunities for modeling and practice.**

   a. Pay staff to attend PD sessions to boost attendance.

   b. Include modeling, hands-on practice, and feedback for trainees; all of these are highly valued by staff.

   c. Track staff training attendance to reduce instances of repeated trainings.

   d. Consider virtual self-paced training modules paired with live check-in sessions to help accommodate staff schedules.

Engaging Families to Support Children's SEL

OST programs regularly attempt to engage families; making SEL a part of that engagement might give caregivers greater insights into SEL goals and practices. OST program leaders (and their OSTIs) can take the following actions:

1. **Develop a family outreach plan.**

   a. Plan for when and how to engage families; family engagement might be more successful after staff have had sufficient time to implement SEL.

   b. Translate family materials as needed and budget for family events and incentives like food to encourage attendance.

2. **Use multiple approaches to engage families in supporting children's SEL.**

   a. Use multiple communication methods and platforms to inform families about SEL (e.g., program calendars, in-person touchpoints, newsletters, bulletin boards).

   b. Use regular in-person contact with families as an opportunity to highlight SEL content (e.g., explaining take-home SEL activities or spotlighting youth SEL projects) and engage families in short SEL rituals.

   c. Provide families with specific SEL strategies, such as conversation starters at pickup to greet their children, or SEL-themed activities like writing a family story to encourage relationship-building.

Improving SEL Quality Using a CQI Process

OST programs can adopt CQI practices to determine the fidelity and quality of their SEL programming delivery (e.g., instruction, rituals, training) and modify approaches as needed. OST program leaders (and their OSTIs) can take the following actions:

1. **Start by collecting a narrow set of data related to the program's SEL goals.**

   a. Focus data collection efforts on data that are relevant to the program's specific SEL goals. For example, if a program's goal is for 80 percent of instructors to deliver explicit SEL instruction at least once a week during afternoon meeting, then a program may want to conduct observations of afternoon meetings.

2. **Review data regularly to track SEL implementation and use data to create action plans for improvement.**

   a. Develop a plan that includes cycles for data collection, analysis, and interpretation, and use this plan to provide structure and accountability.

   b. Establish standing staff meetings to discuss SEL, review data, and track progress against goals.

   c. Allocate time for staff with data expertise to lead and manage collection, analysis, and use of data.

Ways OSTIs Can Support SEL in OST Programs

Effective implementation of SEL programming takes time, capacity, and resources. OSTIs or similar external organizations (such as mayor's offices, district afterschool offices, or other youth-based networks) can provide critical support to OST programs. OSTIs can take the following action:

1. **Work with OST programs to determine what kind of support is most valuable. OSTI support might include**

   a. assistance to OSTs in developing SEL program goals to guide both SEL delivery and the CQI process

   b. connecting OST programs to external SEL resources that OST programs might not have access to on their own (e.g., content expertise, funding)

c. identifying, adapting, or developing SEL instructional materials for OST programs to implement in their programs (e.g., SEL rituals or curricula)

d. offering SEL trainings and coaching

e. providing tools for data collection or analysis.

ABBREVIATIONS

APT	Assessment of Program Practices Tool
AQuA	Afterschool Quality Advancement
CASEL	Collaborative for Academic, Social, and Emotional Learning
COVID-19	coronavirus disease 2019
CQI	continuous quality improvement
NIOST	National Institute on Out-of-School Time
OST	out-of-school time
OSTI	out-of-school-time intermediary
PD	professional development
PSELI	Partnerships for Social and Emotional Learning Initiative
SEL	social and emotional learning
SEL PQA	Social and Emotional Learning Program Quality Assessment

ENDNOTES

1   Damon E. Jones, Mark Greenberg, and Max Crowley, "Early Social-Emotional Functioning and Public Health: The Relationship Between Kindergarten Social Competence and Future Wellness," *American Journal of Public Health*, Vol. 105, No. 11, 2015; Stephanie M. Jones and Jennifer Kahn, "The Evidence Base for How We Learn: Supporting Students' Social, Emotional, and Academic Development," *WERA Educational Journal*, Vol. 10, No. 1, 2017; Terrie E. Moffit, Louise Arseneault, Daniel Belsky, Nigel Dickson, Robert J. Hancox, HonaLee Harrington, Renate Houts, Richie Poulton, Brent W. Roberts, Stephen Ross, Malcolm R. Sears, W. Murray Thomson, and Avshalom Caspi, "A Gradient of Childhood Self-Control Predicts Health, Wealth, and Public Safety," *Proceedings of the National Academy of Sciences*, Vol. 108, No. 7, 2011.

2   Damon E. Jones, Mark Greenberg, and Max Crowley, "Early Social-Emotional Functioning and Public Health: The Relationship Between Kindergarten Social Competence and Future Wellness," *American Journal of Public Health*, Vol. 105, No. 11, 2015.

3   Collaborative for Academic, Social, and Emotional Learning, "Equity Connections to SEL Competencies," webpage, undated. As of August 22, 2022: https://drc.casel.org/sel-as-a-lever-for-equity/equity-connections-to-sel-competencies/

4   Stephanie M. Jones, Katharine E. Brush, Thelma Ramirez, Zoe Xinyi Mao, Michele Marenus, Samantha Wettje, Kristen Finney, Natasha Raish, Nicole Podoloff, Jennifer Kahn, Sophie Barnes, Laura Stickle, Gretchen Brion-Meisels, Joseph McIntyre, Jorge Cuartas, and Rebecca Bailey, *Navigating SEL from the Inside Out—Looking Inside & Across 33 Leading SEL Programs: A Practical Resource for Schools and OST Providers, Preschool and Elementary Edition, Revised and Expanded Edition*, Easel Lab at the Harvard Graduate School of Education, 2021.

5   Noelle Hurd and Nancy Deutsch, "SEL-Focused After-School Programs," *Future of Children*, Vol. 27, No. 1, Spring 2017.

6   Pam Loeb, Stacia Tipton, Erin Wagner, Lynn Olson, Bibb Hubbard, Windy Lopez-Aflitto, and David Park, *Out-of-School Time Programs: Paving the Way for Children to Find Passion, Purpose & Voice—National Surveys of K–8 Parents, Teachers, and Program Providers*, Learning Heroes, Edge Research, September 2021.

7   Collaborative for Academic, Social, and Emotional Learning, "Fundamentals of SEL," webpage, undated. As of May 19, 2022: https://casel.org/fundamentals-of-sel/. This is CASEL's updated definition as announced in October 2020; see Nick Woolf, "CASEL Releases New Definition of SEL: What You Need to Know," webpage, Panorama Education, undated. As of November 27, 2022: https://www.panoramaed.com/blog/casel-new-definition-of-sel-what-you-need-to-know.

8   Adam Tyner, *How to Sell SEL: Parents and the Politics of Social-Emotional Learning*, Thomas B. Fordham Institute, August 2021.

9   Karen L. Bierman, John D. Coie, Kenneth A. Dodge, Mark T. Greenberg, John E. Lochman, Robert J. McMahon, and Ellen Pinderhughes, "The Effects of a Multiyear Universal Social–Emotional Learning Program: The Role of Student and School Characteristics," *Journal of Consulting and Clinical Psychology*, Vol. 78, No. 2, 2010; Adele Diamond and Kathleen Lee, "Interventions Shown to Aid Executive Function Development in Children 4 to 12 Years Old," *Science*, Vol. 333, No. 6045, 2011; Joseph A. Durlak, Roger P. Weissberg, Allison B. Dymnicki, Rebecca D. Taylor, and Kriston B. Schellinger, "The Impact of Enhancing Students' Social and Emotional Learning: A Meta-Analysis of School-Based Universal Interventions," *Child Development*, Vol. 82, No. 1, January/February 2011; Noelle Hurd and Nancy Deutsch, "SEL-Focused After-School Programs," *Future of Children*, Vol. 27, No. 1, Spring 2017; Stephanie M. Jones, Sophie P. Barnes, Rebecca Bailey, and Emily J. Doolittle, "Promoting Social and Emotional Competencies in Elementary School," *The Future of Children*, Vol. 21, No. 1, 2017; Megan M. McClelland, Shauna L. Tominey, Sara A. Schmitt, and Robert Duncan, "SEL Interventions in Early Childhood," *The Future of Children*, Vol. 27, No. 1, 2017; Joseph Durlak and Joseph Mahoney, *The Practical Benefits of an SEL Program*, Collaborative for Academic, Social, and Emotional Learning, 2019; and Joseph L. Mahoney, Joseph A. Durlak, and Roger P. Weissberg, "An Update on Social and Emotional Learning Outcome Research," *Phi Delta Kappan*, Vol. 100, No. 4, 2018.

10   Stephanie M. Jones, Katharine E. Brush, Thelma Ramirez, Zoe Xinyi Mao, Michele Marenus, Samantha Wettje, Kristen Finney, Natasha Raish, Nicole Podoloff, Jennifer Kahn, Sophie Barnes, Laura Stickle, Gretchen Brion-Meisels, Joseph McIntyre, Jorge Cuartas, and Rebecca Bailey, *Navigating SEL from the Inside Out—Looking Inside & Across 33 Leading SEL Programs: A Practical Resource for Schools and OST Providers, Preschool and Elementary Edition, Revised and Expanded Edition*, Easel Lab at the Harvard Graduate School of Education, 2021.

11   Heather L. Schwartz, Laura S. Hamilton, Susannah Faxon-Mills, Celia J. Gomez, Alice Huguet, Lisa H. Jaycox, Jennifer T. Leschitz, Andrea Prado Tuma, Katie Tosh, Anamarie A. Whitaker, and Stephani L. Wrabel, *Early Lessons from Schools and Out-of-School Time Programs Implementing Social and Emotional Learning*, RAND Corporation, RR-A379-1, 2020. As of October 10, 2022: https://www.rand.org/pubs/research_reports/RRA379-1.html

12   Stephanie M. Jones, Katharine E. Brush, Thelma Ramirez, Zoe Xinyi Mao, Michele Marenus, Samantha Wettje, Kristen Finney, Natasha Raish, Nicole Podoloff, Jennifer Kahn, Sophie Barnes, Laura Stickle, Gretchen Brion-Meisels, Joseph McIntyre, Jorge Cuartas, and Rebecca Bailey, *Navigating SEL from the Inside Out—Looking Inside & Across 33 Leading SEL Programs: A Practical Resource for Schools and OST Providers, Preschool and Elementary Edition, Revised and Expanded Edition*, Easel Lab at the Harvard Graduate School of Education, 2021.

13   Collaborative for Academic, Social, and Emotional Learning, *SEL 3 Signature Practices Playbook: A Tool That Supports Systemic SEL*, 2019.

14   Stephanie Jones, Rebecca Bailey, Katharine Brush, and Jennifer Kahn, *Kernels of Practice for SEL: Low-Cost, Low-Burden Strategies*, Harvard Graduate School of Education, December 2017.

15   Stephanie Jones, Rebecca Bailey, Katharine Brush, and Jennifer Kahn, *Kernels of Practice for SEL: Low-Cost, Low-Burden Strategies*, Harvard Graduate School of Education, December 2017.

16   Centers for Disease Control and Prevention, *School Connectedness: Strategies for Increasing Protective Factors Among Youth*, U.S. Department of Health and Human Services, 2009; and Stephanie Jones, Rebecca Bailey, Katharine Brush, and Jennifer Kahn, *Kernels of Practice for SEL: Low-Cost, Low-Burden Strategies*, Harvard Graduate School of Education, December 2017.

17   Stephanie Jones, Rebecca Bailey, Katharine Brush, and Jennifer Kahn, *Kernels of Practice for SEL: Low-Cost, Low-Burden Strategies*, Harvard Graduate School of Education, December 2017.

18   Collaborative for Academic, Social, and Emotional Learning, *SEL 3 Signature Practices Playbook: A Tool That Supports Systemic SEL*, 2019.

19   Collaborative for Academic, Social, and Emotional Learning, *SEL 3 Signature Practices Playbook: A Tool That Supports Systemic SEL*, 2019.

20   Michelle Kehoe, Helen Bourke-Taylor, and David Broderick, "Developing Student Social Skills Using Restorative Practices: A New Framework Called H.E.A.R.T.," *Social Psychology of Education*, Vol. 21, 2018.

21   Collaborative for Academic, Social, and Emotional Learning, *SEL 3 Signature Practices Playbook: A Tool That Supports Systemic SEL*, 2019; and Jordan A. Carlson, Jessa K. Engelberg, Kelli L. Cain, Terry L. Conway, Alex M. Mignano, Edith A. Bonilla, Carrie Geremia, and James F. Sallis, "Implementing Classroom Physical Activity Breaks: Associations with Student Physical Activity and Classroom Behavior," *Preventive Medicine*, Vol. 81, 2015.

22   Susan E. Rivers and Marc A. Brackett, "Achieving Standards in the English Language Arts (and More) Using the RULER Approach to Social and Emotional Learning," *Reading and Writing Quarterly*, Vol. 27, Nos. 1–2, 2010.

23   Elaine M. Allensworth, Camille A. Farrington, Molly F. Gordon, David W. Johnson, Kylie Klein, Bronwyn McDaniel, and Jenny Nagaoka, *Supporting Social, Emotional, and Academic Development: Research Implications for Educators*, University of Chicago Consortium on School Research, 2018; and Nicholas Yoder, *Teaching the Whole Child: Instructional Practices That Support Social-Emotional Learning in Three Teacher Evaluation Frameworks*, American Institutes for Research, January 2014.

24   Candice R. Stefanou, Kathleen C. Perencevich, Matthew DiCintio, and Julianne C. Turner, "Supporting Autonomy in the Classroom: Ways Teachers Encourage Student Decision Making and Ownership," *Educational Psychology*, Vol. 39, No. 2, 2004.

25   Vicki Zakrzewski, "How to Integrate Social Emotional Learning into Common Core," Berkeley Blog, January 22, 2014. As of March 12, 2020: https://blogs.berkeley.edu/2014/01/22/ how-to-integrate-social-emotional-learning-into-common-core/

26   Stephanie M. Jones, Katharine E. Brush, Thelma Ramirez, Zoe Xinyi Mao, Michele Marenus, Samantha Wettje, Kristen Finney, Natasha Raish, Nicole Podoloff, Jennifer Kahn, Sophie Barnes, Laura Stickle, Gretchen Brion-Meisels, Joseph McIntyre, Jorge Cuartas, and Rebecca Bailey, *Navigating SEL from the Inside Out—Looking Inside & Across 33 Leading SEL Programs: A Practical Resource for Schools and OST Providers, Preschool and Elementary Edition, Revised and Expanded Edition*, Easel Lab at the Harvard Graduate School of Education, 2021; Joseph A. Durlak, Roger P. Weissberg, Allison B. Dymnicki, Rebecca D. Taylor, and Kriston B. Schellinger, "The Impact of Enhancing Students' Social and Emotional Learning: A Meta-Analysis of School-Based Universal Interventions," *Child Development*, Vol. 82, No. 1, 2011; and Joseph A. Durlak, Roger P. Weissberg, and Molly Pachan, "A Meta-Analysis of After-School Programs That Seek to Promote Personal and Social Skills in Children and Adolescents," *American Journal of Community Psychology*, Vol. 45, Nos. 3–4, 2010.

27   Second Step, "Second Step Out-of-School Time: A Time to Thrive Together," undated. As of December 12, 2022: https://www.secondstep.org/ out-of-school-time-program; RULER, "Out-of-School Time Resources," 2022. As of December 12, 2022: https://www.rulerapproach.org/how-it-works/ out-of-school-time/; Wings for Kids, homepage, 2022. As of December 12, 2022: https://www.wingsforkids.org/; Growing Sound, "Before the Bullying," undated. As of December 12, 2022: https://growing-sound.com/ before-the-bullying/; Girls on the Run, homepage, 2022. As of December 12, 2022: https://www.girlsontherun.org; and Stephanie M. Jones, Katharine E. Brush, Thelma Ramirez, Zoe Xinyi Mao, Michele Marenus, Samantha Wettje, Kristen Finney, Natasha Raish, Nicole Podoloff, Jennifer Kahn, Sophie Barnes, Laura Stickle, Gretchen Brion-Meisels, Joseph McIntyre, Jorge Cuartas, and Rebecca Bailey, *Navigating SEL from the Inside Out—Looking Inside & Across 33 Leading SEL Programs: A Practical Resource for Schools and OST Providers, Preschool and Elementary Edition, Revised and Expanded Edition*, Easel Lab at the Harvard Graduate School of Education, 2021.

28   Linda Darling-Hammond and Channa M. Cook-Harvey, *Educating the Whole Child: Improving School Climate to Support Student Success*, Learning Policy Institute, September 2018; and Julie A. Marsh, Susan McKibben, Heather J. Hough, Michelle Hall, Taylor N. Allbright, Ananya M. Matewos, and Caetano Siqueira, *Enacting Social-Emotional Learning: Practices and Supports Employed in CORE Districts and Schools*, Policy Analysis for California Education, April 19, 2018.

29   Stephanie M. Jones and Jennifer Kahn, *The Evidence Base for How We Learn: Supporting Students' Social, Emotional, and Academic Development*, Aspen Institute, September 13, 2017; and National Commission on Social, Emotional, and Academic Development, *From a Nation at Risk to a Nation at Hope: Recommendations from the National Commission on Social, Emotional, and Academic Development*, Aspen Institute, 2019.

30   Linda Darling-Hammond, Maria E. Hyler, and Madelyn Gardner, *Effective Teacher Professional Development*, Learning Policy Institute, 2017.

31   Michelle I. Albright and Roger P. Weissberg, "School-Family Partnerships to Promote Social and Emotional Learning," in S. L. Christenson and A. L. Reschly, eds., *Handbook of School-Family Partnerships*, Routledge, 2010; and Megan M. McClelland, Shauna L. Tominey, Sara A. Schmitt, and Robert Duncan, "SEL Interventions in Early Childhood," *The Future of Children*, Vol. 27, No. 1, 2017.

32   National Institute on Out-of-School Time, "Measuring OST Success," webpage, 2022. As of October 17, 2022: https://www.niost.org/Tools-Training/measuring-ost-success

33   The Forum for Youth Investment, "Assessments," webpage, undated. As of October 17, 2022: https://forumfyi.org/weikartcenter/assessments/

34   Partnerships in Education and Resilience, "The Holistic Student Assessment (HSA)," webpage, undated. As of October 17, 2022: https://www.pearinc.org/holistic-student-assessment

35   Aperture Education, homepage, 2022. As of October 17, 2022: https://apertureed.com/

36   SEL Dallas, *SEL Dallas Implementation Guidebook 2020–2021*, 2020. As of November 30, 2022: https://seldallas.org/wp-content/uploads/2021/01/SEL-Dallas-Guidebook-2020_FINAL.pdf

37   Paul Youngmin Yoo, Anamarie A. Whitaker, and Jennifer Sloan McCombs, *Putting Data to Work for Young People: A Ten-Step Guide for Expanded Learning Intermediaries*, RAND Corporation, TL-350-EHC, 2019. As of October 7, 2022: https://www.rand.org/pubs/tools/TL350.html

38   Julie Spielberger, Jennifer Axelrod, Denali Dasgupta, Christine Cerven, Angeline Spain, Amelia Kohm, and Nicholas Mader, *Connecting the Dots: Data Use in Afterschool Systems*, Chapin Hall at the University of Chicago, 2016.

39   Collaborative for Academic, Social, and Emotional Learning, "CASEL Schoolwide SEL Walkthrough Protocol," webpage, 2019. As of October 17, 2022: https://schoolguide.casel.org/casel-lsi-walkthrough/

Ingram Content Group UK Ltd.
Milton Keynes UK
UKHW050758170423
420288UK00002B/8